IN
AMERICAN
HISTORY

DESERT STORM— THE FIRST PERSIAN GULF WAR IN AMERICAN HISTORY

Debra McArthur

Enslow Publishers, Inc.

40 Industrial Road   PO Box 38
Box 398   Aldershot
Berkeley Heights, NJ 07922 Hants GU12 6BP
USA   UK

http://www.enslow.com

*This book is gratefully dedicated to the men
and women who have served the cause of freedom
through their service in the United States military.*

Library of Congress Cataloging-in-Publication Data

McArthur, Debra.
    Desert storm—the first Persian Gulf War in American history /
Debra McArthur.
        p. cm. — (In American history)
    Summary: Recounts the 1991 military action of the United States and
its allies against the forces of Iraqi President Saddam Hussein, relating
historical reasons for the war and reactions of combatants.
    Includes bibliographical references and index.
    ISBN 0-7660-2149-1
    1. Persian Gulf War, 1991—Juvenile literature. [1. Persian Gulf War,
1991.] I. Title. II. Series.
    DS79.723.M38 2004
    956.7044'2—dc22

                                    2003013460

Printed in the United States of America

10 9 8 7 6 5 4 3 2 1

To Our Readers: We have done our best to make sure all Internet Addresses in this
book were active and appropriate when we went to press. However, the author and
the publisher have no control over and assume no liability for the material available
on those Internet sites or on other Web sites they may link to. Any comments or
suggestions can be sent by e-mail to comments@enslow.com or to the address on
the back cover.

Illustration Credits: AP/Wide World Photos, p. 25; Enslow Publishers,
Inc., pp. 6, 20, 92; United States Department of Defense, pp. 10, 13, 35,
38, 46, 49, 50, 54, 62, 64, 71, 77, 79, 82, 87, 88, 97, 99.

Cover Illustration: United States Department of Defense.

★ CONTENTS ★

1 Baghdad Blasted   7

2 Rumors of War   18

3 Preparing for War   32

4 Raising the Shield   42

5 Ready . . . Set . . . Wait   53

6 War From the Air   66

7 One Hundred Hours
     to Victory   80

8 Incomplete Victory?   96

   Timeline 109

   Chapter Notes 113

   Further Reading 124

   Internet Addresses 125

   Index 126

In August 1990, Iraq invaded its neighbor, Kuwait, then threatened to invade Saudi Arabia.

BAGHDAD BLASTED

"At 1:00 A.M. we could hear the roar of jet engines."
—Sergeant Hugh Grossman[1]

American Sergeant Hugh Grossman and his fellow soldiers of the 403rd Military Police Reserve unit lay awake, too tense to sleep, past midnight on January 17, 1991. Time was running out. The United Nations had given Iraqi President Saddam Hussein one last chance. He must remove Iraqi troops from the neighboring country of Kuwait by midnight, January 15, or the United Nations coalition forces would attack. Hussein refused. Grossman and thousands of other military men and women who made up the allied troops stood on the brink of war.

From a military apartment complex called Khobar Tower in Dhahran, Saudi Arabia, the men of the 403rd heard nearby King Fahd airbase roar to life. "It sounded like the whole base took off," Sergeant Grossman recalled. "We watched from the open window as planes took off two at a time."[2]

In the Red Sea and the Persian Gulf, crews of several United States ships awaited their orders. They knew that the steel boxes on their decks held Tomahawk Land

Attack Missiles, known as TLAMs. Each TLAM would fly at an altitude of less than one hundred feet above the ground to reach its target. A radar system on each missile would record the contours of the land it flew over. A microcomputer inside the eighteen-foot-long missile would compare those images to the digitized maps in its memory to keep the missile on course. Navy designers said a TLAM could travel over five hundred miles and still strike within fifty feet of its target.[3] At 1:37 A.M. Baghdad time, the radioman on the *U.S.S. Wisconsin* in the Persian Gulf heard this message: "Alpha, alpha. This is the *Paul F. Foster*. Happy trails."[4] It meant that the first TLAMs had left their ships, traveling towards Baghdad, Iraq.

Tension in the Air

In Saudi Arabia, military men and women in all branches of the service and from many countries were ready for battle. During the five months of Operation

---

SOURCE DOCUMENT

THE LIBERATION OF KUWAIT HAS BEGUN. IN CONJUNCTION WITH THE FORCES OF OUR COALITION PARTNERS, THE UNITED STATES HAS MOVED, UNDER THE CODE NAME OPERATION DESERT STORM, TO ENFORCE THE MANDATES OF THE UNITED NATIONS SECURITY COUNCIL.[5]

On January 16, 1991, White House Press Secretary Marlin Fitzwater read this statement from President George Bush on American television.

Desert Shield, the United States and its allies built up a combined military force in the Middle East to protect Saudi Arabia. Now, hundreds of pilots reviewed flight plans, checked equipment, and verified their targets. Thousands more military personnel at bases in Saudi Arabia prepared for the coming allied attack.

Military leaders worried about Saddam Hussein's response. He had used poisonous gas in the past. Intelligence reports suggested that he was also developing biological weapons that carried disease, or germ warfare. Allied troops were ready for the possibility that he would use those deadly weapons now. Sergeant Grossman's unit practiced the gas attack drill. They had timed drills to see how quickly they could put on the heavy suits and gas masks they hoped would protect them from chemical attack. "That evening we were told to get into our MOPP [Mission-Oriented Protection Posture] gear," he said.[6] MOPP level 3 included a hood, mask, and vinyl shoes. MOPP level 4 was when a soldier also put on his or her gloves.

Sergeant Anita Porter also arrived in Saudi Arabia on the eve of the war. Her first night in Saudi Arabia was a reminder of the terrifying possibilities of war:

> I had just gotten to my unit by dinnertime. I went with someone to eat and got back to unpack. Not long after, we heard the first alarm to alert us of a possible chemical attack. I had not received any briefing by this point. Everyone froze. They instantly began to don their protective masks and get into MOPP 4. I followed a friend to a small bunker. The silence in the bunker was eerie. The only sound that could be heard

*Four soldiers from the 82nd Airborne Division walk around
their camp wearing rain suits, gloves and M-17A1 protective
masks as they try to acclimate their bodies to the heat of the
Saudi summer during Operation Desert Shield.*

was the popping noise from the filters in our gas
masks. It was dark in the bunker, except for a small
flashlight which illuminated the wide eyes of the
soldiers sitting around me. I suppose everyone
thought the same things I did. . . . *This is for real! Not
a training situation! Will we really be gassed? Will we
make it home?*[7]

Instant Thunder

The first attack, code-named "Instant Thunder," was
designed to surprise and cripple Iraq's military forces.
American E-3 Airborne Warning and Control System

(AWACS) surveillance aircraft flew near Iraq's border with Saudi Arabia. The crews watched for Iraqi air traffic. The AWACS flew the same routes they had been flying for the past five months during Operation Desert Shield. Iraqi radar operators were used to these patterns, so the AWACS's movements did not seem strange to them.

Two groups of Air Force Pave Low helicopters took off from Al Jouf airbase in Saudi Arabia. They flew low over the desert to avoid Iraqi radar. Equipped with night-vision technology and satellite navigation systems, they led the first air mission into Iraq. The Pave Lows guided two squadrons of Army Apache helicopters, code-named Team White and Team Red. The Apaches had the firepower to destroy the two Iraqi radar units near the border—radar that could warn Baghdad of the coming attack. The crews in the Pave Lows dropped glowing markers to guide the Apaches. They turned back as the Apaches continued on toward the radar stations.

As Team White approached its target, the radar station's lights went out. The Forward-Looking Infrared Radar System (FLIRS) projected a greenish glow from the heat of the radar antennas and generators of the station. Inside his Apache helicopter, Lieutenant Colonel Dick Cody pulled the trigger to release the first Hellfire missile at 2:38 A.M. Chief Warrant Officer Dave Jones remarked from the seat behind Cody, "This one's for you, Saddam."[8] During the next four minutes, the teams fired Hellfire missiles and seventy-millimeter rockets. They destroyed both radar stations.

Invisible Invaders

The American F-117A Stealth fighter-bombers were designed to be invisible to radar, but the new technology had not been used enough to be sure. EF-11A Ravens flew ahead of the F-117As into the air over Baghdad. These unarmed jets used electronic equipment to jam radar signals.

Although the Ravens successfully jammed the radar, their jamming signals warned the Iraqi defense systems that the city was under attack. Immediately, the Iraqis fired anti-aircraft artillery (AAA) into the air above the city. When the F-117As arrived at 2:58 A.M., the sky above Baghdad looked like a fireworks display. Although the Iraqis could not see what they were firing at, they released hundreds of missiles. Fortunately, the F-117As were high enough to avoid the AAA. They fired their laser-guided bombs at their targets: communications centers, military command posts, and the air defense center.[9] In Washington, D.C., it was 7:00 P.M. Eastern Standard Time.

Window on the War

Some Americans watching television that night already knew Baghdad was under attack. ABC news correspondents from Baghdad had already reported seeing explosions. It was the first time in history that the opening battle of a war was carried live on television.

An air-to-air right side view of an F-117A stealth fighter aircraft of the 37th Tactical Fighter Wing. The aircraft is en route to Saudi Arabia during Operation Desert Shield.

More than 61 million American households were watching it, the most ever for any single broadcast in TV history.[10]

Keeping the television broadcasts coming would be a challenge. As the F-117As were dropping bombs, the TLAMs also arrived. Some TLAMs carried one thousand-pound explosive warheads aimed at military and political command posts. One of the first targets was the Iraqi International Communications Center. It was nicknamed the AT&T building by the American military because it was the central facility for telephone service in Baghdad. At 3:10 A.M. General Norman

Schwarzkopf wrote in his log, "03:10: PHONES OUT BAG."[11] Most television and radio correspondents in Baghdad went off the air when the telephone center was hit by bombs from the F-117As.

CNN scored the winning points in news coverage that night. CNN executives had arranged with the Iraqi government for a special phone line with a satellite connection that did not have to be routed through the telephone center. Obtaining that line had not been easy, however. Ed Turner, CNN's executive vice president said, "We became the biggest nuisances the Iraqi government ever saw until the arrival of the U.S. Air Force."[12] As a result, CNN remained on the air when the other networks were disconnected. As the bombs began to fall, CNN correspondents Peter Arnett, Bernard Shaw, and John Holliman described the live view of AAA explosions. They held microphones out the window of their hotel room to capture the sounds of surface-to-air missile fire. Other TV networks even bought permission to broadcast CNN's news reports in place of their own.[13]

Other TLAMs called Kit 2s carried thousands of tiny spools of carbon threads. The TLAMs were programmed to fly over Iraqi power plants and release the spools. The spools would unwind the carbon filament and short out the transformers. The resulting power failure would cut communication between Saddam Hussein and his troops and disable the air defense system. When the Kit 2s hit Iraq's main power plant at Beiji, the carbon strands caused all six of its generators to shut down. Soon, the Douri power plant and the gas turbine power plant at Taji were victims of carbon filament strands. Within an hour after the telephone center was destroyed, the lights went out in Baghdad. CNN, however, remained on the air for fifteen more hours. Angry that the attack was being broadcast worldwide, the Iraqi government finally shut CNN's broadcast off.

Help From Around the World

American pilots did not work alone in the attack on Iraq that night. British Tornado fighter planes bombed Iraqi airfields. They created craters in the runways to prevent Iraqi fighter jets from taking off. Saudi, French, and Italian fighter planes joined the assaults on Iraqi missile sites. Kuwait's air force hit Iraqi military targets inside Kuwait. Of course, aircraft from all these nations were different. Some were nearly identical to planes flown by the Iraqis. To prevent shooting down a friendly craft, the coalition used electronic codes called Identification Friend or Foe (IFF). Developed by the British, IFF codes had been used since World War II. Before firing on any aircraft, a pilot had to confirm the IFF code of the craft.

Although Iraq's air force was the sixth largest in the world, it had little opportunity to fight on the morning of January 17. With runways blasted and communications disabled, only twenty-five Iraqi aircraft were launched in response to the allied attack, and eight of those were shot down.[14]

"A Great Plan"

In the command center in Riyadh, Saudi Arabia, General Schwarzkopf and his staff waited anxiously to see how Instant Thunder would work. Colonel Harvey D. Watson, deputy director of War Plans and Policy on Schwarzkopf's staff, was cautiously confident about its success. "We had a great plan and had run the plan through all sorts of simulations to help us see if there was anything we had forgotten," he said. "It was scary not knowing how things would go, or how many planes we would lose the first night."[15]

As it turned out, Instant Thunder was one of the most successful air campaigns ever launched. Schwarzkopf expected that as many as seventy-five planes would be shot down in the opening attack. General Charles Horner, the designer of Instant Thunder, estimated that one hundred coalition planes might be destroyed. Other military analysts thought those predictions were far too low. When the sun rose over Baghdad on January 17, over one thousand individual missions, or sorties, had been flown by coalition forces. Eight search-and-rescue helicopters had been sent into Iraq to search for downed pilots, but none had anyone to rescue. One allied pilot, Lieutenant Commander Scott Speicher, was shot down, and presumed dead.[16]

At about 4:30 A.M., the second wave of F-117s approached Baghdad for the next attack. Pilot Al Whitley could see the long lines of car headlights on the highway as the citizens of Baghdad fled the city.

According to Colonel Whitley, the traffic looked "like the interstate from Los Angeles to Las Vegas on a Friday night."[17] At dawn, American B-52 bombers, flown from Barksdale Air Force Base in Louisiana, arrived in the Gulf, armed with cruise missiles aimed at targets in both northern and southern Iraq. The allies had shown Saddam Hussein and his people that the coalition of nations would not stand for his aggression against his neighbor Kuwait.

RUMORS
OF WAR

Iraq is an ancient land with a history of war and conquest. The ancient Greeks called the area between the Tigris and Euphrates rivers Mesopotamia. It is sometimes called the Cradle of Civilization, because the first great civilizations had lived there. Iraqi legend identifies a location near the town of Qurna as the site of the Garden of Eden in the Bible. The Bible does not reveal the location of the Garden of Eden, so this claim cannot be proven.[1] Although Mesopotamia was the target of many invaders throughout history, it was of little interest to most of the world until the discovery of its most abundant natural resource: oil.

Oil and Power

By 1901, oil had been discovered in Persia (now called Iran). Great Britain made an agreement to pay Persia to allow British companies to pump and market the oil. By the beginning of World War I in 1914, the switch from coal to oil as the fuel for warships made oil critical for world power. Also by that time, great amounts of new oil had been discovered in Persia, and the British-run Anglo-Persian Oil Company had begun production at a refinery in Abadan.[2]

During World War I, the use of tanks and airplanes further increased the need for oil by the world's major armies. The British knew they would need more oil than they could get in Persia. When they discovered that the Ottoman Turks were fighting on the side of Germany in the war, they sent troops into Basra, in modern-day Iraq, and gained control of the area. In a 1916 agreement called the Sykes-Picot Agreement, Britain and France divided the Middle East between them. The agreement established Iraq as a country under British control.

The British selected the first king of Iraq, the Arabian prince Faisal. King Faisal I ruled over Iraq with the help of the British. Iraq achieved independence and was admitted to the League of Nations in 1932. Faisal discovered the difficulty in ruling Iraq's different ethnic and religious groups.

Nearly all Iraqis are of the Muslim faith, but this has not served to unify the people. Two groups of Muslims, the Sunni Muslims and the Shiite Muslims, have been in conflict for hundreds of years. After the death of the Muslim prophet Mohammed in A.D. 632, the people needed a new religious leader. One group, the Sunni Muslims, thought that the new leader should be elected by the tribal leadership. They chose Abu Bakr to lead them. Another group of Muslims, the Shiites, believed that the new leader must be a descendant of

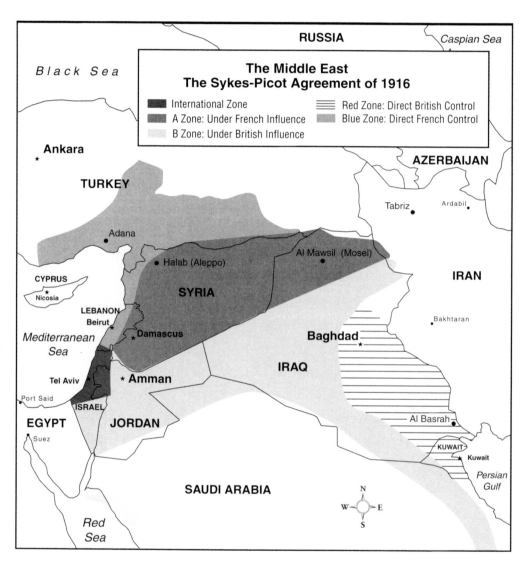

Under the Sykes-Picot agreement, most of Iraq came under
either British influence or control. Here, the divisions of the
agreement are shown on a map of present-day Middle East.

Mohammed. They wanted Mohammed's cousin and son-in-law, Ali, to become the Muslim leader. Ali was murdered by the Sunnis in A.D. 661. The Shiites then selected Ali's son, Hussein, to serve in his place. Hussein was killed in a battle with Sunni tribesmen. The Sunnis then selected their own leader. Ever since, Shiites have believed that Sunnis have ruled over them unjustly.[3] The Sunnis control the capital city of Baghdad in central Iraq. The Shiites live mostly in and around the southern city of Basra.

A separate group of Sunni Muslims, the Kurds, also have lived in the area for many centuries. The Kurds are a non-Arab ethnic group. They are a tribal people, traditionally traveling through the plains of Mesopotamia and the highlands of present-day Turkey and Iran with their herds of sheep and goats. Many live around the city of Mosul in northern Iraq. A 1920 treaty with the allies of World War I promised the Kurds an independent nation in the area where they lived, but Turkey later refused to give up the land within its boundaries, and the British did not want to give up the city of Mosul, which had oil beneath it.[4]

Both the Shiites and Kurds revolted against King Faisal. Faisal recognized that the people had stronger ties to their religious and ethnic groups than to the country. Therefore, they would never be able to unite under one government as one people. Just before he died, King Faisal wrote this message:

> I say, and my heart is full of sadness, that there is not yet in Iraq an Iraqi people, but unimaginable masses

of human beings, devoid of any patriotic idea, imbued with religious traditions and absurdities, connected by no common tie, giving ear to evil, prone to anarchy, and perpetually ready to rise against any government whatever.[5]

The End of British Rule

Faisal's son, Ghazi, became king of Iraq next. Later, his son, Faisal II, became king. During those years, however, the Arab population of Iraq became unhappy with British rule. During World War II, many Iraqis had admired Hitler, because he attacked both the British and the Jews.

After World War II, many Jewish survivors of Adolf Hitler's Holocaust fled to Palestine. On May 14, 1948, the nation of Israel declared its independence as a homeland for the Jews, as recommended by the United Nations. This land in Palestine had previously been occupied by Muslims. The Arab Muslim countries of Egypt, Iraq, Syria, Lebanon, Jordan, and Saudi Arabia refused to recognize Israel. The following day, they attacked Israel. The Israelis fought back, and extended their territory.

In 1958, a group of military officers overthrew Faisal II in Iraq, murdering the royal family. Military leaders took over the power of the government. Several different groups competed for power. Kurds and Shiites continued to fight against the Arab Sunnis for the next ten years. It would take a strong political group to gain lasting control.

The Baath Party in Iraq

After the formation of Israel, a new political party began in Iraq. The Baath party, or Party of Arab Resistance, wanted to unify all Arab states. They wished to throw off British rule and also to return Palestine to the Muslims. They hoped that the death of the pro-British king in 1958 would help accomplish these goals. The new military leaders were part of the Iraqi Communist party. They did not support the goals of the Baathists. The Baathists planned to kill the new leader, Qassem. The plot failed. One of the assassins, twenty-two-year-old Saddam Hussein al-Tikriti, escaped to Syria, then later to Cairo, Egypt.

Over the next few years, Saddam Hussein (the name al-Tikriti means that he came from the city of Tikrit) continued working for the Baath party, even while he remained in Cairo. When Qassem was overthrown in 1963, Hussein returned to Iraq. A distant cousin, General Ahmed Hassan al-Bakr, was among the leaders of the Baath party. Al-Bakr lost favor in the new leadership and was forced to flee the country. The Baathists reorganized outside Iraq and became more powerful.

The Rise of Saddam Hussein

The Baath Arab Socialist Party gained leadership of Iraq in 1968. The Baathist leader, al-Bakr, increased his power by killing anyone who had loyalty to the previous leaders. He made his cousin, Saddam Hussein, chief of internal security. Al-Bakr wanted

Hussein to eliminate all political enemies. Hussein killed thousands of people in public hangings.

Saddam Hussein began using the power and money of Iraq's oil to build up Iraq's military strength. His friendship with the Soviets allowed him to buy Soviet-made weapons. Hussein increased the power of the Iraqi air force with Mirage F1 fighter planes from France. At the same time, he was also building trade with the United States. Eventually, making deals with so many countries backfired. The Soviets backed out of their dealings with Hussein. They refused to supply ammunition for the weapons they had sold him. They also refused to train the Iraqis to service the planes they had sold them.[6]

Meanwhile, Hussein continued his program of killing "enemies." By 1979, he had killed many of al-Bakr's closest advisors and friends by suggesting that they were traitors. Al-Bakr was in ill health and resigned, and Saddam Hussein took control of Iraq. His first act as president was to demonstrate his power by executing one third of the party leadership by firing squad.[7]

Ayatollah vs. "The Great Satan"

As the United States improved relations with Iraq, its relationship with Iraq's neighbor, Iran (formerly Persia), worsened. The Shah of Iran had been a friend of all United States presidents since 1953. Groups within Iran, however, fought to take over the country.

Saddam Hussein

In January 1979, Iran's ruler, the shah, left the country for a "vacation," and never returned.

A religious leader, Shiite Muslim Ayatollah Ruhallah Khomeini, rose up to take the leadership of Iran. Khomeini called America the "Great Satan." Iranians burned American flags and threatened American embassies.

On November 4, 1979, an armed group of Shiites broke into the American embassy in Tehran, Iran's capital city. They took sixty-five people hostage. Thirteen of the hostages were released. The Ayatollah threatened to execute the others as spies. Khomeini held the hostages to show his dislike of President Jimmy Carter. He did not release them until the day Ronald Reagan became president, January 20, 1981. They were held 444 days.

Iran and Iraq at War

In the meantime, Saddam Hussein had his own trouble with Iran. He wanted control of the Shatt al-Arab waterway to the Persian Gulf. Because Iran's cultural heritage is Persian instead of Arabian, Iraq could declare war without angering other Arab nations. Hussein invaded Iran during September 1980. Iran's army was large, but was poorly equipped and poorly trained because of Iran's emphasis on religion instead of military power. Iraq's army, although smaller, had the advantage of modern equipment.

When the war began, the Ayatollah was still holding American hostages. American leaders feared that

Iranian victory would spread anti-American feeling throughout the Middle East. The United States decided to support Iraq in the war. America granted food shipments on credit so that Iraq could keep putting its money into the war effort. It also worked to block sales and shipment of American-made ammunition and replacement parts to Iran.[8]

The Iran-Iraq war was a long and bloody conflict. Iranian peasant soldiers as young as twelve years old ran through mine fields in suicide missions. The troops behind them advanced over the dead children toward the enemy. Saddam Hussein used mustard gas bombs that cause blistering of the skin and lungs to kill and terrorize the enemy.

The Rise of Hussein's Republican Guard

After several humiliating defeats, Hussein tried a new plan. He enlisted young men for his small but highly trained fighting force, the Republican Guard. Because members of Hussein's elite forces were given privileges denied other citizens, this offer was attractive to ambitious young men.

With new jets and tanks, Hussein's Republican Guard began a new war campaign. They attacked Iranian oil plants and ports in the Persian Gulf. Finally, the Iraqis fired Soviet-made missiles into Tehran, the capital of Iran. The Ayatollah could not protect his people. Many Iranian soldiers deserted their units. They lost confidence in their leaders. They left the battlefield and returned home to their families.

In July 1988, Ayatollah Khomeini accepted a cease-fire to end the war. The Iranian army had been reduced to a fraction of its previous strength. The Iraqi army had grown to become the world's fourth-largest fighting force.

At the end of the war, Hussein turned his anger against the Kurds. In the 1970s, the Kurds had tried to withdraw from Iraq to form their own nation. The Iranians had supported the Kurds in their rebellion. Now, Hussein destroyed their villages and used mustard gas bombs on them. Amnesty International, a human-rights organization, estimated that Hussein killed five thousand Iraqi Kurds in 1988.[9]

Debt and Envy

When the Iran-Iraq war ended, Iraq was $80 billion in debt. Much of that debt was owed to the country of Kuwait. Kuwait's land area is only 6,879 square miles, slightly smaller than New Jersey. In 1990, it was one of the richest countries in the Persian Gulf. It controlled about $100 billion in foreign real estate and overseas businesses. The royal family and other Kuwaitis held about $50 billion in private investments. This amount of wealth allowed most Kuwaitis to afford mansions, expensive automobiles, and household servants.[10]

To nearly-bankrupt Iraq, this display of wealth was insulting. Additionally, Kuwait's coastline on the Persian Gulf allowed easy shipment of oil. Iraq has almost no Gulf access, except for use of the Shatt al-Arab waterway, the disputed waterway on Iraq's border with Iran.

Hussein announced that he would not pay back his war debt. He accused Kuwait of producing too much oil for sale to western countries, thus keeping the price low. By summer, the price per barrel had dropped from $20.50 to $13.60. Each dollar of price decrease amounted to a loss of $1 billion for Iraq. He also accused Kuwaiti oil-drillers of stealing oil that belonged to Iraq.[11] He claimed that Kuwait was actually a province of the Ottoman Empire, based upon an agreement between the British and the Turks in 1913 which was never approved. As such, Kuwait would have become part of Iraq. Hussein insisted that he had the right to reclaim Kuwait for Iraq—by force, if necessary.

Accusations Turn to Threats

Early in 1990, Hussein worried international diplomats and military leaders with a series of military actions. First, he moved missile launchers within firing range of Syria and Israel. Later, American and British customs agents stopped Iraqi purchases of nuclear triggering devices and parts of rocket launchers. When Hussein threatened another small Arab nation, the United Arab Emirates (UAE), the UAE asked for help from the United States. The United States sent refueling aircraft to the area, but Saudi Arabia and other Arab nations were offended. They felt that Hussein's threats could be handled among the Arab nations and did not require the help of outsiders.[12]

Photographs from spy satellites showed Iraqi troops camped along the Iraq-Kuwait border, but most nations did not think Hussein would really attack Kuwait. The Defense Intelligence Agency (DIA) watched the daily photos from satellites above the Middle East. On July 21, the photos showed Hussein's Republican Guard gathering along the Kuwait border. On July 24, the satellite photos showed that the assembled troops were large enough to attack Kuwait at any time without warning.

The next day, the American ambassador to Iraq, April Glaspie, was called to a meeting with Saddam Hussein. Hussein told her that he was still talking with the Kuwaitis to prevent war. After the meeting, Glaspie urged America to step back from the situation to allow the talks to proceed. President George H. W. Bush agreed. Some sources, however, believe that Glaspie suggested to Hussein that the U.S. would not interfere in any conflict between Iraq and Kuwait.[13]

SOURCE DOCUMENT

THE UNITED STATES AND IRAQ BOTH HAVE A STRONG INTEREST IN PRESERVING THE PEACE AND STABILITY OF THE MIDDLE EAST. FOR THIS REASON, WE BELIEVE THAT DIFFERENCES ARE BEST RESOLVED BY PEACEFUL MEANS AND NOT BY THREATS INVOLVING MILITARY FORCE OR CONFLICT.[14]

President George Bush stressed the need for peace in a message to Saddam Hussein, dated July 28, 1990.

"A Battle Plan Taking Shape"

On August 1, the threat of war was real. General Norman Schwarzkopf met with Defense Secretary Dick Cheney and Chairman of the Joint Chiefs of Staff, General Colin Powell. They examined the previous weeks' photos of the Iraqi camps. The tanks and weapons were at the back of the camps, while the soldiers sat near their tents at the front. On August 1, the photos showed the equipment moved next to the Kuwaiti border; the tents were gone. Schwarzkopf knew what that meant: "There was no way to mistake what we were seeing for a mere show of force: this was a battle plan taking shape."[15]

At 2:00 A.M. Kuwait time on August 2, 1990, nearly one thousand Iraqi tanks crossed the border. The troops quickly defeated a Kuwaiti brigade defending the border and continued southward toward Kuwait City. By 5:00 A.M., Iraqi troops reached the north end of the capital city. Republican Guard helicopters approached from the south to keep the Kuwaitis from escaping the city. Other troops cut off escape at the coast. More Iraqi divisions guarded the border to prevent Saudi Arabian troops from interfering. By nightfall, the Iraqi troops had control of the city. Infantry units went through the streets to threaten resistors.[16] Saddam Hussein had the prize he wanted: Kuwait.

3

PREPARING FOR WAR

The United Nations Security Council gathered for an emergency meeting before dawn on August 2, 1990 in New York City. It was just ten hours after the invasion of Kuwait began. The Security Council includes delegates of fifteen nations within the United Nations (UN). Its purpose is to maintain peace and security among nations. The Iraqi delegate to the United Nations, Sabah Talat Kadrat, insisted that the Iraqi troops had been requested by the Kuwaitis, and they would leave as soon as order was restored. He told the Council, "The events taking place in Kuwait are internal matters which have no relation to Iraq."[1] The Kuwaiti delegate, however, called Iraq's invasion "an attempt to overthrow all [Kuwait's] constitutional institutions."[2]

The Security Council adopted Resolution 660, accusing Saddam Hussein of "a breach of international peace and security." It demanded that all Iraqi troops withdraw from Kuwait and return to the positions along the border where they had been August 1.[3] The vote on Resolution 660 was fourteen votes in favor and none against. Yemen, an Arab nation, did not vote.

Strong Words, Strong Actions

The United Nations delegates used strong words to describe Saddam Hussein's actions. Thomas R. Pickering of the United States called the invasion a "heinous act of the use of military force."[4] Sir Crispin Tickell of the United Kingdom said it was "an ugly moment in world affairs."[5]

Nations were willing to back their strong words with action. Iraq took over the government of Kuwait and did not withdraw troops, so the Security Council adopted another resolution on August 6. Resolution 661 called for economic actions against Iraq. Therefore, the nations belonging to the United Nations were expected not to buy any products from Iraq and Kuwait. They also were not to sell any weapons or other products to Iraq and Kuwait, except for medical supplies and food.

All United Nations members agreed to obey Resolution 661, even Japan, which had previously stayed out of Middle Eastern conflicts. Nonmember nation Switzerland joined the cause. Even Cuba and Yemen agreed to support the resolution, even though neither had voted for it. British Prime Minister Margaret Thatcher remarked, "I cannot remember a time when we had the world so strongly together against an action as now."[6]

Arab states in the Persian Gulf also had strong reactions to Iraq's invasion of Kuwait. They had always honored an agreement not to attack each other. Saddam Hussein had broken that agreement with his invasion of Kuwait. With Iraqi forces gathered along the Saudi Arabian border, Hussein was in a position to attack another Arab nation. When the Saudis asked for help, many of their Arab neighbors responded. Twelve Arab states voted to send troops to the area to help hold back Hussein's aggression.[7]

"If You Ask Us, We Will Come"

King Fahd Bin Abdul Aziz Al-Saud of Saudi Arabia was willing to accept the help of his Arab neighbors, but the number of troops, tanks, and aircraft they could send would not be enough to fight Hussein's powerful military. King Fahd agreed to meet with United States Secretary of Defense Dick Cheney, General Norman Schwarzkopf, and other military leaders. They showed the king satellite photos of Iraqi troops along the Saudi border and offered the United States's help. Schwarzkopf explained his plan to send thousands of United States troops to defend Saudi Arabia. Cheney delivered this message from President Bush: "If you ask us, we will come. We will seek no permanent bases. And when you ask us to go home, we will leave." After a brief discussion with his advisors, King Fahd responded simply, "Okay."[8]

Within days, ships began arriving in the Persian Gulf to enforce the United Nations blockade. Australia, France, Britain, Canada, Russia, and the United States sent ships to control products coming in and out of Iraq and Kuwait. Britain and the United States sent fighter aircraft and ground troops to help

General Norman Schwarzkopf, commander, U.S. Central Command, joins King Fahd of Saudi Arabia to conduct a review of international coalition forces united against Saddam Hussein during Operation Desert Storm.

the Saudis and the twelve Arab League nations defend Saudi Arabia.[9]

Despite the commitment of troops from all these countries, the United States's force deployed in the Gulf would be larger than any other country's, including the combined forces of the Arab League.[10] Was the United States military ready for this challenge?

The Ghost of Vietnam

The Vietnam War in the 1960s and early 1970s was a grim chapter in American military history. Many

Americans did not like the United States's involvement in the war between North Vietnam and South Vietnam. Young people on college campuses across the country held protest rallies against the war. Although some young men volunteered for service, many were drafted into the Army against their will. Some even chose to leave the country to avoid military service. By the time President Richard Nixon withdrew troops from Vietnam, more than fifty-five thousand Americans were dead. Americans were tired of war.

The Army had problems with crime, racial violence, and lack of discipline. Drug use among soldiers was serious. Around 40 percent of Army personnel stationed in Europe after the Vietnam War admitted using drugs, and 7 percent were addicted to the drug heroin. Many soldiers had little education. Almost 40 percent of enlisted men had no high school diploma, and 41 percent were classified as "Category IV," a classification showing low mental ability.[11] Pay was so low for soldiers that many had to take second jobs or even apply for food stamps to provide for their families. Public opinion was also at an all-time low. According to a 1973 survey, most Americans respected soldiers only slightly more than sanitation workers.[12]

America's Wake-Up Call

In April 1980, the United States military tried to rescue American hostages who had been captured in Iran. It was a bitter failure. Eight soldiers were dead, many more injured. News footage of burning American aircraft wrecked in the desert showed the bad state of the military. It was the wake-up call needed to get America's armed forces moving again. Creating a new American military would not be easy.

First, the image of the American soldier needed to be improved. The "Be All You Can Be" recruiting campaign of the army invited young men to better themselves physically and mentally with military service. In the army, young men could serve both their country and themselves. Better salaries and money for college made the offer even better. Over the next ten years, these changes helped the military. By 1990, 98 percent of enlisted men had high school diplomas, with 75 percent rated in the top two mental ability categories, and 41 percent enrolled in the Army college fund program. Drug abuse among enlisted men dropped from 40 percent in 1975 to less than one percent.[13]

New Technology for a New Era

Along with the higher quality of soldiers came the need for better war technology. Presidents Carter and Reagan supported spending for new military equipment and weapons, despite criticism for it. Critics made fun of the new inventions, especially when they failed in testing. Both the Patriot missile and the M-1 tank failed many times in testing. Harold Brown, secretary of defense under Jimmy Carter, defended the program, saying, "The fact that the systems work is the result of a lot of elaborate testing, during which a lot of things go wrong—which fosters the idea it's all a lot of junk. But you test so you find out what needs to be improved."[14] The same developments that critics laughed at—stealth technology, satellite imaging, and sea-launched cruise missiles, as well as the Patriot missile and M-1 tank—were needed for a modern military campaign.

Another breakthrough was the development of "smart" bombs that could find their targets better than the humans who fired them. During World War II, most bombs hit within one mile of their target. During the Vietnam War, accuracy increased to about

M-1A1 Abrams main battle tanks of Company A, 3rd Battalion, 32nd Armored Regiment, 1st Calvary Division, test their guns prior to taking part in an exercise during Operation Desert Shield.

one quarter of a mile. The infrared targeting system that guided the smart bombs of 1990 could place a bomb within thirty feet of its target.[15]

Training for the Twenty-First Century

Of course, even the best equipment is useless to a soldier not trained to use it. In past wars, death rates in first invasions by United States troops have been high, because pilots and soldiers were not prepared for the battle situations they faced. In 1981, the Army opened its National Training Center (NTC) in Fort Irwin, California, to give soldiers realistic training to prepare them for battle.

Laser-targeting technology with a computer monitoring system (like those used in laser tag games) had just been developed. They allowed combat units to engage in realistic war games. "Kills" by both rifles and tanks could be counted electronically. The opposing forces (OPFOR) were two United States army battalions stationed at NTC. They trained more than 200 days a year to fight against the visiting units who came for training. The OPFOR units attacked using battle plans the Soviets had used. After each battle, commanders watched the game replayed on video screens. They analyzed the strengths and weaknesses of their strategies. The OPFORs were hard to beat. Commanding officers were defeated more often than they won. Through their NTC training, leaders grew smarter and stronger.[16]

Internal Look

Eventually, computer simulations challenged the highest levels of military command. In July 1990, officers of United States Central Command (CENT-COM), a group of top commanders of all branches of the military, played their annual computer-generated war game, Internal Look. Originally, the game was planned to be a battle between United States forces and Soviet forces in the Zagros Mountains of Iran. As Hussein began making threats, Schwarzkopf changed the plan for the war game. He made the game a defense of Saudi Arabia from a Middle East invader such as Iraq.

Schwarzkopf arranged for the officers to receive Internal Look messages about the movements of the fictional invading troops, so they could plan their own troops' movements. As the game went on during the days between July 23 and July 28, 1990, the actual movements of Saddam Hussein's troops were very close to the actions of the game. The messages for Internal Look had to be stamped "Exercise Only" in large letters, so the commanders would not mistake them for real events.[17]

The commanders learned that victory over the Iraqi army could only happen if enough defensive ground troops were in place before Iraq attacked. In the simulation, Iraqi troops advanced far into Saudi territory before they were stopped. In order to be successful, the United States Armed Forces would need the cooperation of the Saudi government. They would

SOURCE DOCUMENT

THE GENERAL WAS A GENIUS. HE CHANGED THE WHOLE WAR PLAN FROM A DEFENSE AGAINST THE RUSSIANS INVADING THROUGH IRAN TO SEEK A WARM WATER PORT ON THE PERSIAN GULF TO A DEFENSE OF THE SAUDI OIL FACILITIES ... WE THEN HAD THE OPPORTUNITY TO REHEARSE THE PLAN ... A MONTH BEFORE WE HAD TO EXECUTE FOR REAL. WHAT AN UNUSUAL OPPORTUNITY. WHAT TIMING.[18]

Colonel Harvey Watson, deputy director of War Plans and Policy, was impressed with the way General Schwartzkopf prepared for Operation Desert Storm.

need to create a plan to transport great numbers of ground forces and equipment quickly to the area.[19]

When Cheney, Schwarzkopf, and the military experts met with King Fahd, they had the plan they needed. After the king granted permission, Cheney gave the go-ahead to begin the plan. Schwarzkopf turned to General Chuck Horner, who had troops standing by, ready to travel to Saudi Arabia. "Chuck," he said, "start them moving."[20]

4

RAISING THE SHIELD

"If there was going to be a U.S. military response, most people I knew in the military wanted to be part of it."

—Major Rhonda Cornum[1]

About two hundred thousand Iraqi soldiers camped near the Kuwait-Saudi border with their tanks. They loaded chemical weapons in plain view. Their presence showed that Saddam Hussein wanted to keep control of Kuwait. At the time of the Kuwaiti invasion, Hussein had closed the borders of Iraq and Kuwait. This stranded thousands of people from other countries. United Nations resolution 664 called for the immediate release of these foreigners. Instead, Hussein announced that these foreign "guests" would be moved to military sites. They would be human shields to prevent those sites from being bombed.

Most military men and women were willing to go to the Middle East. The armed forces of 1990 had changed from that of the past. Many soldiers had children. Many soldiers were women. In 1990, the Department of Defense did not know how many families included two parents in the military. It estimated that sixty-five thousand soldiers were single parents. Soldier-parents would have to make arrangements for the care of their children while they were overseas. They had to make arrangements for guardianship in case they were killed in action.[2]

Major Rhonda Cornum and her husband were both flight surgeons in the Army. When her unit was ordered to go to the Gulf, she never hesitated. Her fourteen-year-old daughter, Regan, supported her decision. "Everyone, even my own daughter, expected me to go to Saudi Arabia," said Major Cornum, "and I would have found some way to get there, even if I hadn't been asked."[3]

The first priority was the military personnel and equipment needed to turn back an attack by Iraqi forces. The Internal Look plan showed an immediate need for one hundred twenty thousand soldiers, led by at least fifteen generals. Schwarzkopf knew his well-trained and well-equipped troops could stand up to the challenge. "We had all the force we needed," he said. "There was only one small problem: the force was still in the United States."[4]

Schwarzkopf's Moving Man

Saudi Arabia was nearly eight thousand miles from the United States. Moving enough soldiers, weapons, and equipment to Saudi Arabia would be like trying to move all the people of a large city, along with all their cars, clothing, phones, computers, food, medical supplies, and other needs. Iraqi troops were already in position to attack Saudi Arabia. Thousands of soldiers in the United States were ready to go; getting them to Saudi Arabia was the challenge. This job would require strong leadership, dedicated soldiers, support from United States civilians, and a fair amount of luck.

General William Pagonis took charge of moving Operation Desert Shield, as this military action was called, to Saudi Arabia. Schwarzkopf called him "an Einstein at making things happen."[5] Pagonis had recently completed a training program called RE-FORGER. In it, planners like Pagonis had to create a plan to move soldiers and equipment overseas quickly.

Pagonis now had to make a similar plan to present to King Fahd. Pagonis would need to show how he would move everything to Saudi Arabia, what ports and roads he would use, as well as what Saudi help he would need. Schwarzkopf presented Pagonis's ideas to King Fahd on August 6. When the king gave his permission and President Bush gave the order to deploy, troops in the United States were ready to board planes, and ships were already on their way to the Gulf.

A Leader of Leaders

The well-trained Saudi soldiers were dedicated to defending their homeland, but they were not experienced. Military commanders from Arab nations and all the coalition nations would need to work together. Only a strong leader could make that happen.

Operation Desert Shield needed Saudi help for success. Transport ships and planes would require seaports and airfields. Soldiers and equipment would need transportation to their bases in Saudi Arabia. Schwarzkopf needed someone who could cooperate and communicate with Saudi military officers. He chose Lieutenant General John Yeosock to be the Central Command Army commander. Yeosock would coordinate army forces to build a defensive shield against Iraqi invasion.

Yeosock had served as a project manager with the Saudi Army National Guard several years earlier. He knew how to work with Saudi military leaders, and he had earned their trust. Before the first soldiers arrived, Yeosock must know where he would station them, and have buses and trucks waiting to take them to a Saudi base.

The "Ready Brigade" of the 82nd

At 9:00 P.M. Eastern Standard Time on August 6, Staff Sergeant John Ferguson's phone rang at Fort Bragg, North Carolina. His unit, the second brigade of the Army's airborne division, the 82nd Airborne, was the "ready brigade." This meant that they were always to be ready to ship out at any time. Soon, each soldier received a call. By 11:00 P.M., the street outside the brigade headquarters was crowded with cars. The second brigade would begin flying out the morning of August 8, although it would take several days to airlift all twenty-three hundred men. The first and third brigades of the 82nd would fly out later.[6]

When Iraq invaded Kuwait on August 2, several United States Navy ships were already on patrol in the

Lieutenant General John J. Yeosock, commander of the 3rd U.S. Army and Army Forces, U.S. Central Command, receives an update on the ground war at the Army Command Operations and Intelligence Center during Operation Desert Storm.

Persian Gulf. They carried cruise missiles, but they did not have fighter airplanes on board. The nearest aircraft carriers were the *Independence*, in the Indian Ocean, and the *Dwight D. Eisenhower*, anchored off the coast of Italy. Each ship carried eighty fighter planes. On August 6, they were both ordered to the Middle East. On August 7, two more ships, the aircraft carrier *Saratoga* and the battleship *Wisconsin*, left the United States on their way to the Gulf.

While the first troopers of the 82nd Airborne were flying toward Saudi Arabia on August 8, the first fighter jets, F-15 Eagle fighters arrived there. The American surveillance aircraft E-3 AWACS also arrived that day and began their routine of flying near the Saudi-Iraq border, patrolling the skies.

A Message to Hussein

When the first soldiers of the 82nd Airborne arrived at the Dhahran airport on August 9, Hussein knew it. CNN carried the event on live television. Hussein and his staff monitored CNN around the clock, so they were sure to see the broadcast. The 82nd Airborne's mission was to defend the airfield at Dhahran. As a paratrooper unit, the 82nd did not have the heavy equipment needed to destroy the Iraqi tanks if they decided to cross the border. Still, the 82nd was backed by enough fighter jets and armed ground vehicles to fight against an Iraqi attack.

The Americans, led by Colonel Ron Rokosz, were excited to be there. According to Colonel Harvey D.

Watson, their confidence was obvious, even to the Iraqis: "Imagine 2500 infantry soldiers holding up the American flag in front of 4,000 Iraqi tanks that might continue south into Saudi Arabia. . . . August 1990 was pretty exciting for those guys."[7]

Their confidence was also contagious. In the days following Iraq's attack on Kuwait, thousands of Saudi workers had left the area, fearing attack. With the arrival of the 82nd, many of them now returned to work.

Many Soldiers; Not Enough Planes

As more soldiers were called up, the biggest challenge became transportation. The soldiers were ready to go. They also needed food, supplies, bottled water, tents, communications equipment, and weapons. Schwarzkopf received angry telephone calls from commanders who could not get men and supplies on planes to the Middle East. A commander at Fort Bragg complained, "I'm sitting here looking at an empty airfield. I've got troops lined up waiting, and there isn't a single airplane anywhere!"[8]

On August 18, President Bush activated the Civilian Reserve Air Fleet (CRAF). By law, the president could require commercial airlines and delivery systems to provide planes in a military emergency. No president had activated the CRAF since Congress passed the CRAF provision in 1952. Both United Parcel Service (UPS) and Federal Express (FedEx) offered cargo planes. Within twenty-four hours, passenger airlines provided thirty-eight jets with four crews each. According to a defense analyst, "We faced up to the most mind-boggling logistics problem ever thrown at us in many years. We came through. The system responded."[9]

Heavy Equipment on the Way

With men and light equipment on the way, the next job was transporting heavy equipment like tanks and trucks. Fortunately, the Marines had several "prepositioning" ships near enough to reach the Gulf in seven days. The ships carried tanks, weapons, and ammunition. They also had enough supplies for sixteen thousand men for thirty days. On August 15, the ships met up with troops of the 7th Marine Brigade, which

Troops march in formation after disembarking from a Civil Reserve Air Fleet (CRAF) Boeing 747 aircraft upon their arrival in support of Operation Desert Shield.

had flown in from Hawaii. Other transport ships were on the way from the United States.

Reservists Called to Join the Shield

The United States armed forces were better equipped and better trained than at any time in history.[10] They were also much smaller than they had been before the Vietnam War. During the 1970s, United States military leaders decided to reduce the size of the active military and increase the size of the reserves and National Guard. Reservists are not on active duty. Instead, they train one weekend a month and one two-week period each year. By law, the president can call up

Military trucks are unloaded from the nose ramp of a C-5A Galaxy transport aircraft of the U.S. Air Force Reserve, Military Airlift Command, in support of Operation Desert Shield.

two hundred thousand reservists for up to six months without the approval of Congress. In the Persian Gulf War, 70 percent of the manpower would come from the National Guard and reserves.[11]

Help from Corporate America

The military's first problem was a shortage of food. The government had developed packaged food for troops called Meals, Ready to Eat (MREs). It did not have enough to feed the soldiers already in Saudi Arabia, however. To solve the problem, the army bought canned, single-serving packaged meals like Dinty Moore and Lunch Bucket. By the end of the war, the Army had purchased nearly 24 million of these meals from American companies.[12] The army also purchased food from local businessmen in the Middle East.

Soldiers also needed uniforms. Desert Shield soldiers each needed four desert battle dress uniforms in the "chocolate chip" camouflage pattern. The army had enough material for two hundred thousand uniforms. It needed nearly six hundred thousand. Wrangler Jeans, American Apparel, and other manufacturers agreed to sew uniforms. Even with this help, they could not produce enough uniforms before the war was over. Many soldiers went to the desert in dark green uniforms.[13]

"The Aluminum Bridge"

Within two weeks of the decision to send troops to Saudi Arabia, over seventy thousand troops were in

SOURCE DOCUMENT

I FIRMLY BELIEVE THAT WE ARE GOING TO WAR. I ALSO BELIEVE THAT THIS IS TOTALLY NECESSARY. HUSSEIN IS A MAN WITHOUT A CONSCIENCE AND MUST BE STOPPED . . . I AM READY TO GO.[14]

Major Michael Donnelly of the Air Force's 10th Tactical Fighter Squadron wrote in his journal about his feelings on the possibility of war.

place. Many more were on the way. They included not only pilots and soldiers, but also doctors, mechanics, truck drivers, telephone installers, and many more. According to the Military Airlift Command (MAC), over one billion pounds of equipment and supplies had arrived or were on the way to Saudi Arabia. At times during the airlift, up to eighty planes were in the air over the Atlantic Ocean at the same time on their way to the Gulf. MAC called it "the aluminum bridge to the Middle East."[15]

There was still much to do. Military leaders feared that Hussein might attack if he felt threatened. Many more troops would be needed, especially if the plan changed from a shield protecting Saudi Arabia to a sword to drive Saddam Hussein out of Kuwait. On August 24, Schwarzkopf prepared to move his headquarters from Washington to Saudi Arabia. There, he would make his plans and wait for war.

READY . . .
SET . . .
WAIT

Rhonda Cornum, a major in the United States army, stepped from the airplane to the concrete runway at King Fahd Airbase in Saudi Arabia on August 25, 1990. A blast of hot air hit her. It seemed to follow her as she walked across the concrete. It felt like exhaust from the airplane's engines, but was actually the desert wind. "Mostly the heat was as dry as a blast furnace," she said, "but when the wind shifted, the humidity from the Persian Gulf covered everything in a smothering blanket of moist air."[1]

Heat and dehydration were two serious dangers for soldiers in Saudi Arabia. Daytime temperatures were over 110 degrees. Training in the intense heat caused the soldiers to lose body moisture in sweat. When they trained with MOPP gear, it was even worse. Water was the single most important supply for the troops. Dehydration could quickly become deadly. The Saudi and Kuwaiti soldiers needed three gallons of water a day to survive. The Americans, who were not used to life in the desert, needed five gallons a day.[2]

Millions of bottles of water were shipped in for the troops. Millions more were supplied by the Saudis. Some soldiers suffered problems from the heat, such as high temperatures, diarrhea, vomiting, and dehydration. Fortunately, they received good care from medical personnel. No American soldiers died from heat stroke. In fact, the numbers of heat-related illness in Saudi Arabia was lower than the usual rate at American military bases in a typical summer.[3]

"The Largest Sandbox in the World"

Sergeant Hugh Grossman's first impression of Saudi Arabia came from his view of it from above. "We flew

Members of an 82nd Airborne Division artillery battery sit on their M-102 105mm howitzers while taking a meal break during Operation Desert Shield.

SOURCE DOCUMENT

WE WERE CONSTANTLY GETTING SAND EVERYWHERE. BEFORE WE COULD LIE DOWN IN OUR SLEEPING BAGS WE HAD TO PICK THEM UP AND SHAKE THEM OUT. WE WOULD GO TO SHOWER, AND BEFORE WE GOT BACK TO THE TENT WE WERE COVERED WITH SAND AGAIN.[4]

Sergeant Jeff Moore of the 270th Transportation Detachment of the 37th Transportation Command explains how difficult it was for soldiers to deal with the sand.

down the Nile River out of Egypt and across the sea to Saudi Arabia. All I could think was it was the largest sandbox in the world."[5] The areas around air bases became cities of tents. At Al Kharj, the powdery sand would not hold tent stakes, so the Army brought in twenty-five thousand truckloads of dirt. The troops set up six hundred tents in twenty-four rows and added a hospital, laundry, stores, and even a Baskin Robbins ice cream shop.[6]

By early September, coalition forces were confident they had enough strength to hold back an Iraqi invasion of Saudi Arabia. Kuwait was still being held by Hussein's forces, however, and the troops did not know whether or when the situation might turn into a war.

Chemical Threat

Besides the work of constructing their base camps, soldiers continued to train for combat. Pilots flew practice missions. Ground troops drilled with tanks and weapons, learning not only how to operate their equipment, but also how to prepare for the worst: chemical or biological warfare.

Hussein had used mustard gas in attacks against the Iranians and the Kurds. Mustard gas is a liquid chemical that can be delivered on a bomb. In an explosion, the liquid scatters and vaporizes into the air. Mustard gas causes skin burns and can burn the lungs if inhaled. It can be fatal.

The Central Intelligence Agency also believed that Iraq had chemical nerve agents such as sarin and tabun that affect the nervous system and can cause a person to become unable to breathe. Gulf War soldiers carried injectors of an antidote to several types of nerve gas.

Spy satellites found more than twenty buildings that looked like refrigerated storage sites for biological weapons. Biological weapons such as botulinum and anthrax are germs that infect the human body. According to the *Journal of the American Medical Association*, a single gram of botulinum could kill up to one million people.[7] Botulinum can be sprayed from an aerosol can or can be delivered in a bomb's warhead. Some soldiers took pills to protect them against biological weapons. Even with these precautions, a soldier's MOPP gear was the best defense against chemical and biological agents.

Machines in the Desert

The sandy desert was hard on equipment. In windy conditions, the sand was blown to altitudes above ten thousand feet. When sucked into the engines of some aircraft, the sand blocked cooling vents. This made the engines overheat. Calcium in the sand damaged the heat-resistant coatings on the fan blades in the engines. Pratt and Whitney, a manufacturer of the engines, imported Arabian sand to the United States to test its engines. General Electric, another engine maker, found a way to wash the blades to prevent problems. It made a video to teach soldiers how to do the same.[8]

The desert also caused problems for ground vehicles. Sergeant Jeff Moore's army transportation unit took care of a fleet of five thousand tractor-trailer trucks used to carry equipment and supplies to bases in Saudi Arabia. The main supply routes (MSRs) were hard-packed, unpaved roads. The trucks were designed for use on paved roads. Driving on the rough MSRs would shake the trucks' parts loose. The heat increased the air pressure in the tires and caused frequent blowouts. Sand, heat, and vibration also damaged the trucks' electrical systems, especially the lights. When the trucks had to travel after dark, the drivers attached light sticks to the back of the trailers. According to Moore: "We would tell the convoy commanders they needed to stop when it started to get dark so the drivers could get out and break the light sticks so they would shine and the drivers could see the trailer in front of them."[9]

When a trailer was dropped off by one truck, it often sank into the sand before the next truck could hitch onto it to take it to its next stop. The soldiers then had to dig ditches under the trailer so that the truck could back down to get its wheels low enough to hitch onto the trailer. The soldiers cut wooden boards to put under the wheels to keep the trailer from sinking. If it rained, the sand would shift, the boards would break, and the trailer would sink again.[10]

Wrestling Fans From Many Nations

The transportation units had challenges with the drivers they employed in Saudi Arabia. Many were from nearby Middle Eastern countries. The army provided them with sleeping quarters on the bases, but the drivers preferred to go home when they finished their routes. If they did not come back the next morning, it could take several days to contact them to come back to the base. The American commanders needed to keep the drivers near.

The foreign drivers were fascinated by the video-tapes of professional wrestlers the American soldiers watched in their off-duty time. When the transportation officers realized this, they set up a tent with a large-screen television. Each morning, they announced the wrestling events for the evening's entertainment. Soon, the drivers were spending their nights at the base, and were ready to drive a new route every morning.[11]

Muslim Laws *Vs*. American Freedom

Some American entertainment was not welcome in Saudi Arabia. Alcoholic beverages were illegal in the country. The strict Muslim laws of the Saudis made it a crime to possess magazines with photos of naked women. In order to keep the good will of the Saudis, Schwarzkopf outlawed alcohol and magazines with nudity on all American military bases.

Some soldiers complained that they had a constitutional right to the same things they could enjoy on a military base in the United States. Schwarzkopf replied:

> I hope you recognize that the Constitution of the United States applies only on U. S. soil, so therefore we don't have any constitutional rights in Saudi Arabia. . . . So just like we require them to obey our laws in the United States, they have every right to require us to obey their laws here.[12]

Another challenge for the cooperation of American and Arabian forces was the presence of female military personnel. Most Saudi women are expected to wear black clothing that covers them completely, including long sleeves, dresses no shorter than the ankles, a shawl over the head, and a veil over the lower half of the face. Women are not allowed to drive cars or to walk in public by themselves. Saudi law put many restrictions on female soldiers. When female soldiers took off their jackets to help unload boxes of supplies, some Saudis complained that the T-shirted women were indecent. Merchants in towns like Dhahran and Riyadh did not like to see off-duty female soldiers browsing in their stores, especially since they, like all soldiers in a war zone, carried their weapons with them at all times.

Over thirty-five thousand American female service members worked as drivers, guards, doctors, and engineers, and filled other essential jobs.[13] Sergeant Anita Porter worked at a printing plant at King Fahd airbase. She sometimes drove into town to take care of business for the plant. She was often stopped at roadblocks. Sometimes Saudi soldiers searched her car. They always let her go after checking her credentials, but she sometimes worried that they would put her in jail. One humorous incident was at first frightening for her:

> Once a truck pulled over as I was just about to enter our company area. Two men jumped out of their truck and were yelling at me. A guard posted at the gate to the compound stopped them, and it was soon apparent what they wanted. They wanted their photo taken with me, because of my blonde hair and blue eyes![14]

Coalition Cooperation

At the end of October, Saddam Hussein still refused to remove his troops from Kuwait. Coalition troops had been deployed only for the defense of Saudi Arabia. Now they might be needed to attack Iraqi troops to drive Hussein from Kuwait. More forces were called to service in the Gulf. This doubled the number of soldiers in Saudi Arabia. Thousands more soldiers came from the United States, England, Egypt, France, Italy, and other nations, in addition to those from Saudi Arabia and Kuwait.

On some bases, soldiers from different countries lived side-by-side. The American pilots of Michael Donnelly's unit got along well with the Italian pilots who lived nearby. As Donnelly and his friends ate their MREs, they could smell the aromas of Italian cooking from the chow tent on the other side of the fence. Donnelly said, "Although we shot frequent yearning looks in their direction, those Italians never invited us over. They had no trouble asking the American female service members to eat, though."[15]

Blues and Boredom

Building up military strength in Saudi Arabia had happened with amazing speed, but diplomats were still trying to convince Hussein to withdraw from Kuwait. By mid-November, the coalition had thousands of soldiers in the desert, but no war for them to fight. According to Colonel Harvey Watson, who served on Schwarzkopf's staff, the soldiers had "six months of hurry up and wait. Morale was still high, but I think the troops began to doubt whether we would really get into a fight, the job they were there to do."[16]

As the seasons changed, so did the weather in the desert. Although daytime temperatures were more pleasant than in the summer, as soon as the sun set, the air turned cold. As the Christmas season approached, soldiers became homesick and bored. They continued their training, but they also had off-duty time. To pass the time, the soldiers watched videos and played table tennis, volleyball, and card games. Cornum's unit found another form of entertainment: spider fighting. "We found a big, ugly, hairy camel spider in the desert and called it 'Kid Bengal.' . . . [W]e put up signs announcing the fights and scoured the desert to find opponents for the Kid, usually other spiders, scorpions, and once a large lizard."[17]

The troops looked forward to cards and packages from home. American support was strong. Many soldiers received encouraging cards from schoolchildren

General H. Norman Schwarzkopf, commander-in-chief, U.S. Central Command (second from right), and other military officials stand by as President George Bush prepares to speak. The president and his wife, Barbara Bush, later had Thanksgiving dinner with members of the 197th Brigade, 24th Infantry Division.

and others through letter-writing campaigns like Operation Dear Abby, in which the popular newspaper columnist forwarded letters from the public to deployed military personnel.

American companies also gave support to soldiers and their families. Toy stores and manufacturers sent Christmas toys to children of soldiers. They sent sports equipment like footballs and Frisbees to Saudi bases. Mary Kay Cosmetics of Dallas, Texas, sent a pink eighteen-wheel truck to Fort Huachuca, in Sierra Vista, Arizona. It carried a shipment of sun block, lip protector, and shaving cream to be sent to soldiers in the Persian Gulf.[18] Yellow ribbons on trees, homes, store windows, and car antennas showed the support of millions of Americans for the military men and women in Saudi Arabia.

Buildup to War

Meanwhile, Saddam Hussein was beginning to feel the pressure of the coalition blockade. In the gulf, coalition ships stopped tanker ships bringing oil from Iraq, cutting off the country's main source of income. Ships carrying military goods and other prohibited cargo bound for Iraq were also stopped and forced to turn back.

Kuwaitis who escaped the country reported that Iraqi soldiers were stealing goods from homes and stores in Kuwait. Petty Officer Second Class Andrew Watson served aboard the *U.S.S. Mississippi*, one of the ships patrolling the Gulf. "We stopped a ship that was

First Lieutenant Kathy Hambleton, the navigator aboard a KC-135 Stratotanker aircraft, checks her charts while on a refueling flight during Operation Desert Shield.

carrying stolen cars from Kuwait," Watson said. "The cargo was headed for Jordan via the Suez Canal, apparently to be sold there. There were still registration papers in the cars for their true owners."[19]

On November 29, the United Nations passed Resolution 678. It allowed the coalition to use military force against Iraq if Hussein did not withdraw from Kuwait by January 15, 1991. A week after the resolution passed, Hussein released the foreign hostages still held in Kuwait and Iraq. Their clothing showed low levels of radioactivity. This suggested that nuclear weapons were present at some of the Iraqi military sites where the hostages had stayed.[20] Hussein still refused to withdraw from Kuwait.

By New Year's Day, it was clear that something would happen soon. Soldiers and pilots began an intensive training schedule. Now that the hostages had been released, Schwarzkopf and his staff no longer had to worry about hurting them. They could now plan their offensive campaign to attack Hussein's Republican Guard and free Kuwait. It was time to unleash Instant Thunder.

6

WAR FROM THE AIR

The Instant Thunder attack on Baghdad on January 17, 1991, proved the power of the coalition forces. The next day, bombers continued taking off from Saudi airbases. Warships in the Gulf launched more Tomahawk Land Attack Missiles (TLAMs) toward targets in Baghdad. Eight B-52 bombers from Michigan arrived and dropped more than a hundred tons of explosives. Seven more B-52s from Louisiana arrived to drop bombs on power plants and communications centers.[1] Operation Desert Storm, as the military action was now called, blew into Iraq ready to damage Saddam Hussein's military.

The Coalition War Plan

Schwarzkopf and the coalition commanders planned to start the war with air attacks and end with the ground war. The air war plan contained three components: the Strategic Air Campaign (SAC), Attainment of Air Superiority, and Battlefield Preparation.[2] The SAC consisted of destroying radar, communications, and military targets like weapons plants and command headquarters. Next, the coalition would destroy

Hussein's planes and airfields so that the coalition air force would have control of the skies. The final part of the air war plan was to attack Hussein's ground forces. They planned to destroy as many tanks and artillery units as possible before the coalition ground troops began the fight to regain Kuwait.

The first night's attack destroyed power plants, communications, and radar in Iraq. The bombing of airfields kept most of Hussein's planes from fighting coalition planes. Within the first few days, coalition radar confirmed that Iraqi planes were flying. However, instead of flying toward battle, they were flying toward Iran, away from the conflict. Iran did not take part in the war, but allowed Iraqi pilots to take their planes there to be out of danger. American pilots called them "the white feather squadron," since they were fleeing for their own protection.[3] Air superiority of coalition forces had been achieved within one week.

Hussein's Revenge

Hussein did not take the insult of the attack on Baghdad lightly. He had launchers positioned in Iraq ready to fire explosive missiles known as Scuds. The Iraqis had purchased Scuds from the Soviets in 1984, during the war with Iran. The Soviet Scuds carried a one-ton warhead and could travel about 180 miles.[4] By 1988, Hussein's engineers had modified the Scuds. Scuds fired at Iran's capital city, Tehran, had traveled nearly 350 miles.[5]

Scuds were not very accurate. Crews aimed them by knowing the direction and distance to the target, then adjusting the angle of the launcher.[6] The explosive power of Scuds varied. Some had smaller warheads and larger fuel tanks for longer range. Military leaders worried that Scud missiles could carry chemical warheads.

At about 3:00 A.M. on January 18, 1991, twenty-five hours after the first attack on Baghdad, American radar detected Scud launches. The United States had Patriot missiles ready to fire at Iraqi Scuds that might be launched toward Saudi Arabia. The Patriots were designed to destroy the Scuds in the air. The idea of firing missiles to destroy other missiles had first been discussed in 1946, right after World War II. General Dwight Eisenhower had described it as "hitting a bullet with another bullet."[7] Some military leaders were doubtful of the Patriots' ability to destroy the Scuds.

The problem on January 18, however, was the target of the Scuds. The Scuds were headed toward Israel where no Patriots protected the cities. Israel was not involved in the conflict between Iraq and Kuwait, but its friendship with the United States made Israel a target. Most important, Hussein knew that Israel had always responded with force whenever it was attacked. If Israel were to attack Iraq, Arab countries would probably withdraw from the coalition rather than fight on the same side as Israel. This would destroy the coalition.

As sirens wailed, Israelis hid in bomb shelters and put on gas masks. Early reports from Tel Aviv, Israel, confirmed six Scuds landing there and two more in Haifa. News sources reported that the bombs contained poisonous gas. Live news broadcasts showed reporters in Tel Aviv wearing gas masks.

Telephone lines between America and Israel were immediately flooded with calls. Thousands were from United States citizens checking on the safety of relatives in Israel. One was from United States Secretary of State James A. Baker III to Israeli Defense Minister Moshe Arens.

"We regret very much what happened," Baker said. He continued:

> This is a formal request to withhold a response. We're outraged by the action that the Iraqis have taken. We're very sad and sorry about the attacks, but we've got aircraft going to the launch sites. . . . I hope you won't respond or retaliate. Please consider this a formal request for moderation.[8]

The reports of poisonous gas were wrong, but buildings were damaged in both Tel Aviv and Haifa. About sixty people had minor injuries, but no one was killed in the attack. Israel sent dozens of warplanes into the skies that night, but they did not attack Iraq. Israel's nuclear weapons were ready, but they were not fired.[9]

For several tense days, Americans and Israelis discussed ways to handle the Scud attacks without an Israeli attack on Iraq. Finally, they reached a compromise. Israel would not attack if the United States would do its best to protect Israel. Squadrons of coalition planes flew continuous night missions over western Iraq searching for mobile Scud launchers mounted on trucks. Although the pilots rarely found a launcher, the missions were watched by Israeli radar. As long as the planes continued to search, the Israelis were satisfied.[10] Patriot missile launchers were sent to Israel.

Ecological Terrorism

Unable to disband the coalition by drawing Israel into the war, Hussein's next weapon was the source of Kuwait's wealth: oil. First, the Iraqis opened oil pumps at a loading dock off the coast of Kuwait. Next, they drained the oil from five Kuwaiti oil tanker ships docked in the Gulf. A Department of Defense report estimated that 7–9 million barrels of oil poured into the waters of the Gulf.[11]

The oil spill threatened military operations. The crude oil on the surface of the water could enter a ship's cooling system and ruin it. In areas where the oil was more than one millimeter thick on the surface of the water, it could burn. Three days after the oil was first released, it caught fire.[12] Black smoke filled the area. In a battle situation, the smoke and heat would interfere with infrared and laser targeting systems.

The immediate concern, however, was the approach of the oil slick toward Saudi power plants and water desalinization plants. The Saudi desalinization facilities removed salt and purified seawater for drinking. They provided most of the drinking water for the coalition troops and the Saudi people.

The oil spill could cause serious environmental damage. Because the Gulf is shallow, it takes a long time for the motion of the tides to take the gulf water out and replace it with new water. The oily muck threatened the lives of sea birds, coral reefs, and sea plants and animals. The Sierra Club, an environmental group, predicted that the damage from the spill, "could destroy the Gulf for decades."[13]

The nearby oil-producing states had equipment to control oil spills, but could not handle a problem this

Black smoke pours from burning oil at an offshore oil terminal near Kuwait City destroyed during Operation Desert Storm.

large. The location of the spill was also a problem. Major General Robert Johnston, chief of staff of the United States Central Command, told the press, "[The spill] is in enemy territory. We can't just go in and shut it off."[14] The Saudis asked for help. An American team of environmental experts went to Saudi Arabia to work with specialists there to help contain the spill and reduce environmental damage.

More Bombs in Baghdad

Over the next five weeks, coalition aircraft continued to bomb Iraqi targets. The bombers destroyed military sites such as command centers and suspected weapons plants and storage areas. The precision laser-targeting systems allowed pilots to destroy a target with little damage to the building next to it. Tanker airplanes refueled fighter jets in the air, allowing pilots to fly more missions each day without landing.

Spy satellites helped locate targets. Observers watched for days or weeks to confirm that the location was used for military purposes. Despite these precautions, some bombing incidents caused concern and criticism. The first was a concrete building in Baghdad known as the Al-Firdos bunker. American intelligence reports showed that the building had been recently fortified with more concrete, enough to protect against nuclear attack. The CIA believed that the building was being used as a command post for Iraqi leaders.

In the first few days of the war, soldiers covered the roof with camouflage to make it harder to spot from the air. Traffic between the bunker and the nearby Iraqi Intelligence Service suggested that Hussein's top men were working there. On February 13, two F-117A jets targeted Al-Firdos and bombed it. Then came a grim discovery: Hundreds of Iraqi civilians were using Al-Firdos as a public shelter.

International news reports showed bodies being removed from the rubble and crying relatives of those killed. Despite the tragedy of civilian deaths, American intelligence leaders still believed Al-Firdos was used by Iraqi military leaders. The presence of computer cables in the wreckage of the building suggested that this might be true. Later evidence showed that the communications equipment was probably used by high-ranking military officers who took shelter at Al-Firdos at night along with their families and other civilians.[15]

Prisoners on TV

Fighter pilots continued to bomb Iraqi targets with great accuracy and with few losses. Although Hussein did not have planes in the air to fight the bombers, he used anti-aircraft artillery (AAA) and surface-to-air missiles (SAMs) against the fighter planes. Coalition bombers knocked out most of Hussein's radar facilities in the first few days of fighting, so AAA and SAMs were mostly fired by human controllers who shot at planes they could see. Although they were not very accurate, they did shoot down some coalition aircraft. Some allied pilots were killed. Others ejected from their planes and were picked up by search and rescue helicopters. Some were captured by the Iraqis and kept as prisoners of war.

The prisoners held in Iraq were beaten by guards. They were forced to appear on television and make statements against the coalition's attack on Iraq. Saddam Hussein threatened to use them as human shields. Instead of persuading the nations of the coalition to end the war, it angered them and made them more determined than ever to stop Hussein.

America Watching

News coverage played a more important role during the Persian Gulf War than it had ever played in any previous war. Americans could watch around-the-clock coverage of bombings, military press briefings, and reporters roaming the streets of Baghdad. With the superiority of coalition airpower and the low casualty rate of both coalition troops and Iraqi civilians, most Americans supported the war. One public opinion poll showed that 84 percent of Americans approved of President George Bush's handling of the war.[16]

Not all Americans were in favor of the war. As the January 15 deadline approached, protestors began to pound drums in the park across the street from the White House. "I hear that George Bush hears the drums and is disturbed," said one protestor. "I hope he gets the message. If you are killing, you are against God."[17] Demonstrators who believed that America's main reason for war with Iraq was our need for oil carried signs with slogans like "No Blood for Oil."

As the war began, many of those who had objected to it still supported the men and women who served. A shopkeeper in Connecticut took down the peacerally signs she had placed in her windows earlier. "It's not of my choosing, but we're in a full-fledged war," she said. "We should get on with it."[18]

The Media and the Military

Coalition leaders watched CNN in their command posts. Saddam Hussein and his military aides also relied on CNN for news. Over sixteen hundred reporters traveled to the Middle East.[19] Both sides tried to influence news coverage and use it to their advantage. CNN reporters broadcast from a bombed-out factory targeted as a chemical weapons plant. Iraqi officials put up large signs, in both English and Arabic, which identified the building as a "Baby Milk Plant." One plant worker wore a shirt with "Baby Milk Plant Iraq" printed in English.[20]

SOURCE DOCUMENT

THIS WAS THE FIRST US WAR TO BE COVERED BY NEWS MEDIA WHO WERE CAPABLE OF BROADCASTING REPORTS INSTANTANEOUSLY TO THE WORLD, INCLUDING THE ENEMY.[21]

This statement was made in a government publication entitled Conduct of the Persian Gulf Conflict: An Interim Report to Congress.

Coalition commanders knew that Saddam Hussein was watching CNN reports. They used it to give him false information. According to Colonel Harvey Watson, "We used . . . TV coverage of the practice amphibious assaults in the Gulf of Oman when we never had any intent of using amphibs. [Hussein sent] . . . Iraqi divisions along the Gulf Coast thinking we would do an amphib assault to retake Kuwait City."[22] Iraqi troops were sent to defend the Kuwaiti coast. They were pulled away from the locations where ground troops would later attack.

Searching for Scuds

Hussein did not have many planes in the air, but he continued to launch Scud missiles. Coalition planes searched for trucks that carried Scud launchers. Mobile launchers sometimes parked in the middle of neighborhoods or under highway overpasses. The Iraqis also had decoy mobile Scud launchers that looked almost identical to real ones.

The Iraqis could set up and fire the mobile launchers quickly, then move out of the area. Coalition soldiers called it "shoot and scoot."[23] Radar could trace the location of the launch, but as soon as a missile was fired, the mobile launcher was moved. Finding and destroying Scud launchers was one of the greatest frustrations of the coalition forces.

Patriot missiles were not as effective against Scuds as the United States had hoped. Patriots were first made to destroy enemy aircraft, but were modified to use against other missiles. They are not designed to explode when hitting a target. Instead, they were supposed to explode near a target and destroy it with shrapnel, or exploded pieces of itself. The shrapnel did not always destroy the Scuds. In some cases, big pieces of both missiles fell to the ground.[24]

When the Scuds were fired at Israel, Patriot missile crews noticed several strange things on the radar screens. First, the Scuds did not fall straight down; they seemed to spiral to the ground. They also did not show up well on radar and they seemed to contain several missiles, instead of just one.[25]

Military personnel examine a Scud missile shot down in the desert by an MIM-104 Patriot tactical air defense missile during Operation Desert Storm.

Later, Army missile experts realized that Iraqi weapons designers had attached extra fuel tanks to the Soviet Scuds. When each missile came down through the atmosphere, the fuel tanks broke apart from the missile. The Patriot system was made to release two Patriot missiles at each Scud. The radar system picked up each piece of a Scud as a separate missile. It would automatically fire as many as ten Patriots at each group of Scud pieces. By the middle of February, just before the ground war was to begin, supplies of Patriots were running low.[26]

Glad to be on Our Side

The third goal of the air war was for planes to attack Hussein's tanks and vehicles to decrease Iraqi battle strength before the ground war. On February 5, some pilots discovered a new way to destroy Iraqi tanks. The pilots of F-111Fs, F-15Es, and A-6s used Forward-Looking Infrared Radar Systems (FLIRS) to find targets at night. The FLIRS systems targeted objects or people according to temperature. Some Iraqi tanks took positions in the desert where they were partly buried in the sand to hide them from the coalition planes. The Iraqi tanks sat out in the sun all day, absorbing heat. At night, the tanks gave off heat, making them visible to the FLIRS. The pilots then used their laser targeting to bomb the tanks. They called this system "tank plinking."[27]

Sergeant Jeff Moore and the other soldiers at Eagle Base waited near the border to be sent into Iraq. "We

An air-to-air view of a multinational group of fighter jets, including, left to right, a Qatari F-1 Mirage, a French F-1C Mirage, a U.S. Air Force F-16C Fighting Falcon from the 401st Tactical Fighter Wing, a Canadian CF/A-18A Hornet and a Qatari Alpha Jet, during Operation Desert Shield.

would watch the Air Force planes fly over our position heading into Iraq to drop their bombs on the locations where we knew we would soon be," he said. "We were hoping they were hitting their targets. [T]he ground was shaking from the explosions. . . . I was sure glad to be on our side."[28]

7

ONE HUNDRED HOURS TO VICTORY

By the third week of February, the three objectives of the air war had been accomplished. The coalition had control of the air, many military targets in Baghdad were destroyed, and Iraqi ground forces had been reduced. Coalition troops had cut off supply lines to many Iraqi troops. After weeks of tank plinking by coalition pilots, the Iraqi soldiers were afraid to sleep in or near their tanks. They were tired, afraid, and hungry.

The Russians and Iraqis presented a last-minute plan for Iraq to withdraw from Kuwait and avoid a ground war. The coalition rejected it. President Bush presented Saddam Hussein with one last chance to withdraw. The Iraqi Command Council called Bush's deadline "an aggressive ultimatum to which we will pay no attention."[1] February 24, 1991, would be the beginning of the ground war, G-Day.

The Three-Part Attack Plan

The battle plan for the ground war divided the coalition troops into three areas of attack. The battleground was referred to as the Kuwaiti Theater of Operations (KTO). Toward the Gulf Coast, at the east of the KTO, the Marines would fight alongside the soldiers of the Joint Forces Command (JFC). The JFC was made up of Saudi, Egyptian, and Syrian troops. They would move across the Saudi/Kuwaiti border to recapture Kuwait City from the Iraqis.

In the center of the KTO, the Army's VII Corps would cross the Saudi/Iraq border through the front line of the Iraqi troops into southern Iraq. The Iraqi troops at the front of the battlefield were neither well-trained nor well-equipped for battle. The allies believed that these troops would be fairly easy to conquer. Behind these weaker troops, guarding Baghdad, waited Saddam Hussein's strongest troops, the Republican Guard.

The third part of the plan was a surprise attack on the west side of the KTO. For this plan, troops would advance north into Iraq west of the main battle. They would establish a Forward Operating Base (FOB) for attack aircraft. From the FOB, they would take control of the main road between Baghdad and Basra. The coalition was scheduled to begin its attack at 4:00 A.M. on February 24. About six hundred twenty thousand coalition soldiers from thirty-seven countries waited. They were ready to engage five hundred forty-five thousand Iraqi soldiers in combat.[2]

G-Day: Sunday, February 24, 1991

The Marines of the 6th division crossed the border from Saudi Arabia into Kuwait before 6:00 A.M. on G-day. The Iraqis had buried explosive devices called mines under the sand near the border to prevent the allies from entering Kuwait. The Marines' mission for Sunday was to cross two minefields in southern Kuwait.

The only way to get troops across the minefields was to make the mines blow up without causing harm to anyone. The Marines used ropes of explosives called line charges. One end of the line charge was attached

Members of the Coalition forces drive a captured T-72 main battle tank along a channel cleared of mines during Operation Desert Storm.

to a rocket. When fired from a launcher, the rocket would drag the line behind it. The line would land on the ground across the area where the mines were buried. When the Marines blew up the line charge, it would cause the mines beneath it to explode. After exploding the mines, tanks with plows and rakes crossed the area to find any unexploded mines that might still be there.

On the east and west sides of the Marines, groups of JFC soldiers were performing similar missions. Behind them, the Army's Tiger Brigade, with M-1A1 tanks and night vision capabilities, was ready to fight against the Iraqi army. There was not much of a fight. As the Marines advanced through the minefields, many Iraqis surrendered and most of the Iraqi artillery was destroyed. By noon, the Marines had crossed both minefields. They cleared pathways for the tanks of Tiger Brigade to move into Kuwait.

Retreating Iraqi soldiers ignited hundreds of oil wells. The pressure of the rising oil from beneath the earth would cause them to continue to burn until they could be successfully sealed off. Until coalition troops had control of Kuwait, however, the burning oil wells could not be capped.

"PSYOPS Works!"

In the middle of the KTO, the men of the Army's VII Corps were ready to cross the Saudi/Iraq border, marked by a bulldozed ridge of sand called a sand berm. Thousands of Iraqi soldiers hid in bunkers behind the berm. Between bombing raids, coalition planes dropped printed leaflets on the troops.

Sergeant Anita Porter worked in the army's Psychological Operations (PSYOPS) unit. Their print shop created the leaflets. The leaflets had both Arabic and English messages. They showed pictures of Iraqi soldiers being fed and treated kindly by the allies. They encouraged the Iraqi soldiers to save their lives by surrendering.

As soon as the fighting began, thousands of Iraqi soldiers approached coalition troops to surrender. Over fifty-five hundred Iraqi soldiers surrendered in the first ten hours of the ground war. "Many soldiers held the leaflets over their heads as they surrendered," Porter said. "If it weren't for the leaflets many more lives may have been lost. PSYOPS works!"[3]

The large number of Iraqi prisoners of war (POWs) put a strain on soldiers assigned to guard the POW camps. Sergeant Hugh Grossman's camp in Saudi Arabia expected five hundred Iraqi prisoners to arrive the first day of the ground war. That night, twenty-two hundred Iraqis arrived at the camp. Military police checked names against computer records to see if any of the prisoners were wanted for war crimes in Kuwait. Some prisoners carried Rolex watches and cash stolen in Kuwait.[4]

Cobra Strike

As the Iraqi and coalition tanks along the border exchanged fire, more than two hundred fifty thousand

troops, including the British 1st Armored Division
and the French 6th Light Armored Division, along
with the American 82nd Airborne Division and their
tanks and armored vehicles, headed west. The Iraqis
had no planes in the air, and no radar or satellites
watching the troops they fought. They did not see
the coalition troops leaving from the back of the
forces. Later, the troops turned northward across
the Iraqi border.

The French planned to take control of the town of
As Salman and its nearby airfield in order to establish a
Forward Operating Base (FOB) as a refueling and supply base for troops scheduled to attack the Republican
Guard. The FOB, located about sixty miles inside Iraq,
was code-named Cobra. Before noon on G-Day, Cobra
had been secured and was ready to support the Apache
attack helicopters that arrived a few hours later.[5]

As the troops traveled, so did trucks of equipment,
food, fuel, ammunition, and supplies. The line of
trucks was so long that the first vehicles reached Cobra
while the last ones were still in Saudi Arabia.[6] As
Sergeant Jeff Moore's transportation unit drove
through a passage in the border berm carved out by
the Big Red One, the Army's 1st Infantry Division, a
sign greeted them. "Welcome to Iraq! Courtesy of the
Big Red One. Follow the leaders."[7]

G-Day + 1: The Coalition Advances

Monday, February 25, brought rain and fog over the
battlefield, along with black smoke from the burning oil

wells in Kuwait. On the east side of the KTO, the Marines of the 1st Division and JFC troops were moving northward toward Kuwait City. With help from Cobra helicopters, the Marines destroyed over sixty Iraqi vehicles and captured hundreds of prisoners.[8]

On the west side of the KTO, a thousand soldiers of the Army's 101st Airborne Division were ready to head north from FOB Cobra to a point along Iraq's Highway 8 near the Euphrates River. Highway 8 was the main route between Baghdad and the city of Basra. The coalition wanted to take control of the highway, cutting Saddam Hussein's troops off from their commanders in Baghdad. With control of Highway 8, the coalition could also block the escape of the Republican Guard.

The paratroopers of the 101st would land first, to be joined by 3rd Brigade's artillery and missile launchers. The paratroopers landed in mud near the highway. They struggled through knee-deep muck carrying weapons and equipment. Chinook helicopters took off from Saudi Arabia carrying the heavy artillery. As soon as they were unloaded from the helicopters, the vehicles sank axle-deep in the mud. Despite these problems, the Americans secured Highway 8 by sundown.

Tragedy at Al Khobar

When the ground war began, the coalition was more concerned about T-72 tanks than about Scuds. Compared to the high-tech weapons of the coalition,

Military personnel sift through the remains of a warehouse hit by an Iraqi Scud missile Feb. 25, 1991, killing 27 U.S. Army Reserve personnel and wounding 100 others during Operation Desert Storm. The building housed the 475th Quartermaster Group (Provisional).

the Scuds seemed crude and clumsy. Coalition soldiers joked, "How many Iraqis does it take to fire a Scud? Three: one to aim, one to fire, and one to watch CNN to see where it lands."[9] On February 25, however, they learned just how deadly a Scud could be.

At 8:30 that evening, radar showed a Scud headed toward Dhahran Airbase in Saudi Arabia. Several Patriot units tracked the missile, but they were all too far away to fire at it. Because of a computer error, the tracking equipment at Dhahran did not see the

Demolished vehicles line Highway 8, the route fleeing Iraqi forces took as they retreated from Kuwait during Operation Desert Storm.

Scud. A Patriot missile did not fire. The Scud hit a warehouse in the Al Khobar area near Dhahran where American soldiers were living. Twenty-eight soldiers were dead; another ninety-eight were wounded. The software to correct the computer error was on a delivery truck. It arrived the following morning.[10]

G-Day + 2: The Highway of Death

On February 26, planes of the Joint Surveillance Target Attack Radar System (JSTARS) spotted vehicles moving north on Highway 6, from Kuwait City at 1:00 A.M. Iraqi troops were trying to escape from the capital city before coalition troops arrived. Air Force F-15E pilots were sent to stop the convoy along Highway 6. They had just heard the news of the Scud attack on Al Khobar. They were not willing to let the Iraqis escape.[11]

The pilots bombed the vehicles at the front of the line, then bombed the ones at the end of the convoy. Marine and navy pilots helped hit all the vehicles in between. By morning, all six lanes were jammed with burning vehicles. Almost all were civilian vehicles stolen from Kuwait City. News reports would later call Highway 6 the "Highway of Death."

By this time, the Iraqis knew that the Marines were near Kuwait City. Other coalition divisions, including the Tiger Brigade, had closed off the roads leading out of the city. One group of tanks tried to escape through Al Jahrah, but the Tiger Brigade was already there. The Iraqis quickly surrendered. Kuwait was free.

SOURCE DOCUMENT

THERE WERE TANKS THAT WERE BLOWN APART WITH PARTS SCATTERED EVERYWHERE . . . WE SAW BODIES (SKELETONS WITH CHARCOALED SKIN WRAPPED AROUND THEM) STILL SITTING IN TRUCKS WHERE A BOMB HAD GONE OFF BY THEM AND SUCKED THE LIFE RIGHT OUT OF THEM . . . THIS IS NOT THE PRETTIEST SIGHT TO SEE BUT YOU HAVE TO REMEMBER IT WAS WAR, AND THAT IS OUR JOB.[12]

Sergeant Jeff Moore remembers the devastation he witnessed during Desert Storm.

Battle of 73 Easting

The VII Corps in Iraq was not finished with its mission. Coalition forces wanted to be sure Hussein's Republican Guard would no longer be a threat in the Middle East. The VII Corps was joined by the British army. Together they advanced westward to meet the Republican Guard in the southeastern corner of Iraq.

At 7:15 A.M. Tuesday, February 26, a helicopter crew spotted a T-72 tank of the Republican Guard about thirty miles east of the Kuwait border. The 3rd Armored Division moved forward, toward the front line of the Iraqi Tawalkana Division. Thick oil smoke blew westward across the battlefield, along with a fierce sandstorm. Visibility was less than half a mile. The tanks of VII Corps inched forward all day. At 4:00 P.M., VII Corps met the Tawalkana. With their Forward-Looking Infrared Radar Systems (FLIRS), the M-1A1 tanks could target the T-72s long before the Iraqi soldiers could see the coalition tanks.

The tanks fought with the Tawalkana for several hours. So many Iraqi vehicles were burning that the FLIRS screens began to go blank from the heat. Several armored divisions were battling the Tawalkana. In just one of the battles, the Iraqis lost seventy-six T-72s and eighty-four infantry fighting vehicles, as well as artillery equipment and other vehicles. Only four American tanks were destroyed.[13]

G-Day + 3: The Final Battles

February 27 began on a triumphant note: Kuwait liberated from Iraqi occupation. The march into the city was led by the JFC forces. Joyful Kuwaitis met the troops and cheered their parade through the streets. Citizens along the street waved Kuwaiti, American, Saudi Arabian, and other flags as they celebrated.

Elsewhere, the war went on. Republican Guard vehicles were escaping northward from Basra on Highway 6. Apache helicopters flew in to stop them. The pilots attacked the traffic on the two-lane road. Soldiers jumped from the vehicles. Some were shooting at the Apache helicopters. One Air Force F-16 was hit by enemy fire. The pilot ejected from his plane. A Blackhawk helicopter responded to his distress call, but was shot down as it tried to rescue him. Five crewmen aboard the Blackhawk were killed. Three others, including flight surgeon Rhonda Cornum, were captured by the Iraqis. The prisoners would not know for at least two weeks that they were captured on the last day of the war.

The last tank battle against the Republican Guard came at noon on Wednesday. The Madinah division of the guard waited behind a sand berm in the desert, hoping to take the M-1A1s by surprise. The M-1A1s, with their superior equipment, spotted the T-72s and began firing from a distance twice the range of the T-72s' guns. Within forty minutes, the battle was over. More than sixty T-72s had been destroyed. In the final hours of G-Day + 3, the remaining coalition

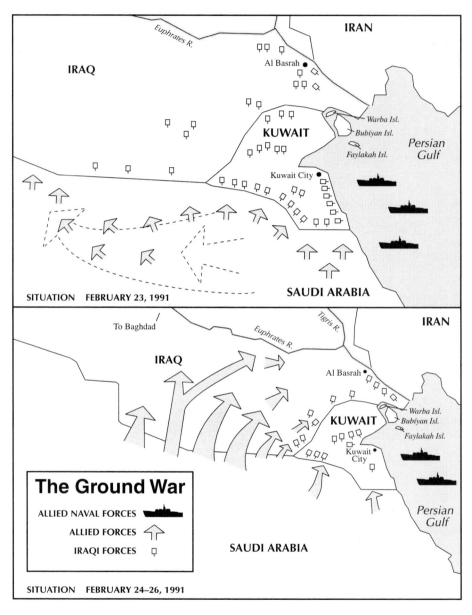

During the ground war, Allied forces overpowered Iraqi
troops in only three days.

troops began moving to surround the enemy before they could escape.[14]

Cease-fire

By Wednesday evening, February 27, photos of the burning vehicles along the Highway of Death reached Washington. News of the last few battles contained the reports of great numbers of surrendering troops. CNN showed destroyed Iraqi vehicles and dead bodies in the desert. Coalition warplanes and tanks continued to chase retreating Iraqi troops to destroy them in their own country. George Bush, Colin Powell, and Dick Cheney were concerned that world opinion would turn against America.

Kuwait was free and the strength of the Republican Guard had been drastically reduced. President Bush and his advisors concluded that the main objectives of Operation Desert Storm had been achieved. On Wednesday evening, President Bush announced to the nation, "At midnight tonight, Eastern Standard Time, exactly one hundred hours since ground operations commenced and six weeks since the start of Desert Storm, all U.S. and coalition forces will suspend offensive combat operations."[15]

On the morning of March 3, General Schwarzkopf arrived at Safwan airfield with other American and coalition military leaders. In a large tent set up for the meeting, they sat across the table from the Iraqi generals. They discussed the conditions for ending the war. Schwarzkopf noted that the only time Iraqi

General Sultan Hashim Ahmed showed emotion was during the discussion of POWs. Ahmed announced that Iraq was holding forty-one coalition POWs. He asked Schwarzkopf how many Iraqis were being held. According to Schwarzkopf, when told there were over sixty thousand, "[Ahmed's] face went completely pale: he had no concept of the magnitude of their defeat."[16] One hour later, the Iraqis came out of the tent and hurried to their waiting vehicles. Schwarzkopf addressed the crowd outside. He announced that the Iraqis had agreed to the terms of the cease-fire agreement.

President George Bush declared the war, " . . . not only a victory for Kuwait, but a victory for all the coalition partners. This is a victory for the United Nations, for all mankind, for the rule of law, and for what is right."[17] Although it was a triumphant moment for America and the coalition, it was also controversial. Many people, including military leaders and the public felt that our mission in Iraq would not be finished until Saddam Hussein was removed from power. In one television interview, Schwarzkopf commented, "Frankly, my recommendation had been . . . continue the march. . . . We could have continued to reap great destruction on them. . . . it's one of those [decisions] that historians are going to second guess forever."[18]

Americans joyfully received the news that the war was over. General Michael Dugan, former U.S. Air Force Chief of Staff, called it "a rapid, total, and remarkably low-cost allied victory," and "a triumph of American air power and American leadership."[19] A few days later, coalition POWs were released. Many of the men who were captured reported being beaten and psychologically tortured by the Iraqis. The two women POWs were not mistreated in this way.

In June 1991, parades in Washington, D.C., New York City, and many towns across America celebrated the victory of America's fighting men and women in the Persian Gulf War. Flags waved, people cheered, and confetti rained down on tanks and Humvees.

In the Middle East, however, the scene was very different. Although he had agreed to the terms of the cease-fire, Saddam Hussein was never forced to admit defeat. Hussein was still in power, and he turned his anger against his own people. Although the Persian Gulf War was officially over, conflict with Saddam Hussein had far from ended.

8

INCOMPLETE VICTORY?

The end of Operation Desert Storm brought mixed emotions. Saddam Hussein did not admit any wrongdoing in his invasion of Kuwait. In his speech to his people at the end of the war, he insisted that Iraq had won the war against the "criminal entity of America and its major allies."[1]

The coalition troops had performed well, but Saddam Hussein was still in power. Had the coalition finished the job?

During the months of Desert Shield and Desert Storm, Iraqi soldiers terrorized the Kuwaitis. They beat those who resisted. They committed public executions in the name of Saddam Hussein. A Pentagon report charged that 1,082 Kuwaiti citizens were killed by the Iraqis during the months Iraq held Kuwait.[2] Kuwait also suffered great damage and destruction to homes, religious shrines, and public buildings. At the zoo in Kuwait City, many animals died of neglect. A bullet was found in the shoulder of an elephant.[3] After the war, the Kuwaitis turned against their own citizens who had cooperated with the Iraqis. They committed public executions and beatings, just as the Iraqis had done.

U.S. Air Force personnel, led by Lieutenant General Chuck Horner, marching in the National Victory Celebration parade honoring the coalition forces of Desert Storm.

Ecological Damage in Kuwait

Kuwait suffered serious and long-lasting ecological damage. Oil fire experts from eighteen countries worked for months in Kuwait to put out the fires. Smoke from the fires blocked sunlight for months. The last of the 613 oil well fires was extinguished on November 6, 1991. According to Green Cross International (GCI), over 60 million barrels of oil were spilled in the desert, contaminating freshwater and soil. About 10 million barrels of oil were released into the Gulf, soiling over nine hundred miles of coast-line. Seven years after the Gulf War, GCI estimated that 40 percent of the freshwater reserves in Kuwait were still contaminated.[4]

Saddam Hussein's Wrath

Conditions were also bad in Iraq. After the war, the Shiite Muslims of southern Iraq and the Kurds of northern Iraq both rose up in protest of Hussein. Some news sources have suggested that President Bush encouraged the CIA to help rebel groups in Iraq.[5]

After the cease-fire, the Republican Guard reorganized to attack the rebels. In the south, Iraqi soldiers used tanks, rocket launchers, and armed helicopters to attack Shiites. Shiites seeking food and protection told coalition troops that the Iraqis had killed thousands. Officially, the American government said it did not want to become involved in the internal affairs of Iraq. American soldiers gave food and water to the Shiites. Later, President Bush allowed the military to enforce a no-fly zone to protect the Shiites against the Iraqi helicopters. The Iraqis responded by attacking the Shiites with ground troops.

In the north, Hussein's troops moved to attack the Kurds who, as they had several years earlier, wanted to withdraw from Iraq and form their own nation. Asaf Muhamad was thirteen years old when the troops invaded his Kurdish town in April of 1991:

> Around 3:00 A.M. we heard noise from the city. I ran out of the house with my family. I could see the city was smoking. We could hear missiles going overhead and bombs exploding all around us. The soldiers were

shooting people for no reason. We passed many dead people in the street. We did not carry anything. We just ran to save our lives. The weather was so cold and snowy. We walked for two days and nights along the road to Turkey, moving to stay away from tanks that came behind us and shot at people.[6]

Coalition troops gave aid to the Kurds. They dropped bundles of food for them, and provided medicine and clothing. They set up aid stations in Turkey to help the Kurds who had left Iraq. The United States

Kurdish children gather around Cmdr. Donald Thurston of Naval Environmental Preventive Medicine Unit 7 (NEPMU-7) as he passes out items from a Meal, Ready-to-Eat (MRE) at a refugee camp near the city of Zakhu. U.S. and coalition troops established the camp as part of Operation Provide Comfort, a multinational effort to aid Kurdish refugees in northern Iraq and southern Turkey.

gave money to Turkey to help the Kurds. A few months later, most Kurds returned to their homes. Saddam Hussein promised that they would not be in danger.

A New Image for America's Military

A hand-drawn cartoon was taped to the wall at the Riyadh Hyatt Regency Hotel where General Schwarzkopf held his press briefings. It pictured a grave in the desert. The tombstone read, "Here Lies Vietnam."[7] The war shaped a new national attitude toward the United States military. In a poll taken by the newspaper *USA Today*, 78 percent of Americans said they had "a great deal of confidence in the military."[8]

America's military in the Persian Gulf War also proved that women could serve in military roles alongside men. Women were not placed in direct combat positions, but they did perform almost all other jobs. They flew helicopters and refueling aircraft, drove trucks, transported enemy POWs, repaired mechanical equipment, and served as air traffic controllers. A Congressional report concluded, "The deployment of women was highly successful and . . . women performed admirably and without significant friction or special considerations."[9]

Many Nations; One Cause

The Persian Gulf War proved that forces from many nations could work together in battle. One analyst called the coalition, "a display of teamwork that skeptics thought would work only in an internationalist's fantasy. In practice, however, the alliance moved as a smoothly coordinated machine."[10] Politically, the unity of the coalition was needed to show Saddam Hussein that his invasion of Kuwait was not acceptable to his Arab neighbors or to the rest of the world.

The Persian Gulf War allowed leaders of many countries to work together. The sensible actions of both American and Israeli statesmen during the Scud attack on Israel prevented the breakdown of the coalition. At the end of the war, the JFC troops led the way into Kuwait City to show the important role of Arabs in freeing Kuwait.

The Media and the War

Although most of the world watched the war as it happened, the news reporters who covered it were not given as much freedom as they had in other wars. The Department of Defense organized "media pools." These groups of journalists traveled together with a military escort. The media pools could not interview soldiers without approval. They were not allowed to travel without their escort. The Department of Defense defended the media pools as being necessary for security of the troops. A soldier who was interviewed could accidentally give away military plans. This was an important consideration, because Saddam Hussein was monitoring American media.

During the Vietnam War, reporters had been able to travel anywhere they were brave enough to go, even to the battlefield. Some people believed that there was too much news coverage in Vietnam. They felt that the scenes Americans saw on television caused the many protests against the war. In the Gulf War, journalists were invited to press briefings where they were told of each day's events. According to one reporter: "They [the Pentagon] restricted our access to a point where we couldn't do any of our own reporting. They fed us a steady diet of press conferences in which they decided was the news would be. And if somehow, after all that, we managed to report on something they didn't like, they could censor it out."[11]

On television, pictures of exploding missiles made it look like Patriot missiles were hitting many Scuds. During the war, the army said that Patriots destroyed 80 percent of Scuds they targeted over Saudi Arabia, and 50 percent over Israel. In fact, most of the explosions were from Patriots hitting the Scuds' fuel tanks. A 1992 government report stated that only 9 percent of targeted Scuds were actually destroyed.[12]

According to some reporters, the public still does not know the whole truth of the Gulf War, and will never know it.

Gulf War Syndrome

One of the most serious controversies of the Gulf War is the number of military veterans who have become ill in the years since the war. Gulf War Syndrome is the name given to symptoms suffered by men and women who served in the Persian Gulf. Some have complained of muscle pain, loss of memory, headaches, joint pain, and other symptoms. According to a 2002 Veterans' Affairs report, as many as 7,758 Gulf War soldiers have died and nearly 200,000 have made medical claims with the Veterans' Administration.[13]

One possible cause of the symptoms may be exposure to chemical agents or the treatments for exposure. To guard against anthrax, many soldiers were given shots to lessen the effects of possible exposure. During the war, chemical alert sirens at military bases often indicated the possible presence of poisonous gasses. Still, officials have always said that no chemical or biological agents were ever released by the Iraqis.

Another possible cause of symptoms could be exposure to radioactive material. The ammunition used by American tanks used depleted uranium to penetrate the armor of the Soviet T-72 tanks. Depleted uranium is the substance left after natural uranium is enriched for use by nuclear power plants. It has lower radioactivity than natural uranium. The military has always insisted that the depleted uranium did not pose a risk for the tank soldiers. Still, some people think that the soldiers may have been exposed to radiation from the tank ammunition.

Many medical studies have been made of Gulf War veterans. Some have shown a higher rate of birth defects in the children of Gulf War veterans than in the general population. Others have shown a higher rate of amyotrophic lateral sclerosis (ALS), also known as Lou Gehrig's disease. It will take many years to know if cancer rates are higher among veterans. Still, the government and the Veterans' Administration are unwilling to admit that these ailments are related to service in the Persian Gulf.

Military Conduct in Question

The conduct of troops in the Gulf War has raised questions about the morality of the coalition's military tactics. Military commanders who saw the pilots' tapes of the attacks along the Highway of Death were disturbed by the killing. The pilots who flew those missions, however, noted that the Iraqis driving along the road were driving stolen vehicles full of stolen property from Kuwait. Also, the many soldiers who jumped out of their vehicles and fled on foot were not attacked.[14]

The day after the attacks along the Highway of Death, the army still wanted to try to destroy as much of the Republican Guard as possible before the war was over. Iraqi Military vehicles headed north from Basra, trying to cross over a marshy area called the Hawr al Hammar. Apache helicopters were ordered to destroy as many of them as possible. Some Iraqi soldiers waved white flags, a sign that they were surrendering. Others fired automatic weapons at the Apaches. Pilots did not know what to do. Should they fire at the soldiers shooting at them, even at the risk of shooting others who might be surrendering? Their commanders told them not to lose any planes. To the pilots, that meant that they should shoot to protect themselves, which would mean that they may have to shoot surrendering soldiers as well as those who were attacking.[15]

As tanks worked to clear paths through the minefields, soldiers in trenches fired at coalition tanks. Armored combat earth-movers (ACEs) worked as bulldozers to flatten out the trenches, burying any enemy soldiers who did not surrender quickly enough. Field officers said that one hundred fifty Iraqi soldiers were buried alive.[16] No loudspeaker warning told the Iraqis to surrender before the ACEs plowed the trenches. Although this policy shocked many people, it was a standard battle tactic used in both World War II and Vietnam. In the late 1970s, a United Nations committee had decided that this was "consistent with the law of war." They made no law forbidding it.[17]

Weapons Inspections

After the war, United Nations weapons inspectors searched Iraq for signs of chemical, biological, and nuclear weapons. At the Iraqi city of Salman Pak, weapons inspectors found evidence of germ warfare research, including anthrax. They could not tell if the Iraqis had actually developed the germs into weapons, or if they had found a way to load them into bombs.[18] The inspectors found seventy tons of nerve gas and four hundred tons of mustard gas that had not been destroyed in the bombings.[19] Iraqis who had fled their country told of nuclear weapons development. In March 1991, the Defense Intelligence Agency predicted that "Iraq could produce a nuclear weapon in two to four years," and had enough aircraft left to use those weapons in a war.[20]

Another War

In May 2002, the United Nations tried to do more weapons inspections. Saddam Hussein insisted that his country was not producing chemical, biological, or nuclear weapons. He would not allow United Nations inspectors into Iraq. During the summer of 2002, war with Iraq again seemed likely. President George Walker Bush, son of the president who had led the coalition during Operation Desert Storm, accused Hussein of cooperating with the terrorist groups believed responsible for attacks on the World Trade Center on September 11, 2001. Bush threatened that if Hussein continued to refuse to allow United Nations inspectors into Iraq, he would be ready to send America's military back to Iraq.

With the threat of military action and a new United Nations resolution, Saddam Hussein agreed to give

SOURCE DOCUMENT

WHILE THERE ARE MANY DANGERS IN THE WORLD, THE THREAT FROM IRAQ STANDS ALONE, BECAUSE IT GATHERS THE MOST SERIOUS DANGERS OF OUR AGE IN ONE PLACE . . . BY ITS PAST AND PRESENT ACTIONS, BY ITS TECHNOLOGICAL CAPABILITIES, BY THE MERCILESS NATURE OF ITS REGIME, IRAQ IS UNIQUE.[21]

President George W. Bush spoke out against Iraq during a speech in Cincinnati, Ohio, on October 7, 2002.

inspectors access to Iraqi facilities. Inspectors arrived November 25, 2002. George W. Bush was convinced that Hussein must be removed from power. Even though weapons inspectors had not found anything, the president was ready to fight. In early November 2002, General Tommy Franks, head of U.S. Central Command, estimated that at least one hundred thousand American troops would be needed to fight a war with Iraq.[22]

At 10:16 P.M. March 19, 2003, Eastern Standard Time, President George W. Bush addressed the nation: "My fellow citizens, at this hour, American and coalition forces are in the early stages of military operations to disarm Iraq, to free its people and to defend the world from grave danger."[23]

He called it Operation Iraqi Freedom. His goal was simple: remove Saddam Hussein from power. Over forty countries joined the coalition to aid in the military operation known as Operation Iraqi Freedom. The opening engagement included a bombing raid on a Baghdad building where intelligence reports said Saddam Hussein might be.

Ground troops invaded Iraq from the south the following day. As in 1991, many Iraqi troops surrendered as coalition troops advanced. Fighting was fierce in some areas, but in some towns, the people welcomed coalition troops and cheered them. On April 4, coalition troops took control of Saddam Hussein International Airport and were advancing towards Baghdad. On April 7, another bombing strike was aimed at Hussein and his sons. There was no evidence that Hussein was killed in that attack. Some rumors hinted that he might have fled to Syria. By April 9, allies declared that the Iraqi government of Saddam Hussein had fallen.

As in 1991, war protestors questioned the president's motives for attacking Iraq. Tests at a warehouse in Iraq in April 2003, showed signs that the building had once contained nerve agents and blistering chemicals. At that time, however, weapons inspections had not yet found any weapons of mass destruction.[24]

What Now?

Operation Desert Storm accomplished its military objectives of liberating Kuwait and reducing the military strength of Iraq's Republican Guard. It also helped the United States military regain the respect of the American public. It allowed many nations to work together to accomplish a common goal. Still, it did not improve the lives of the Iraqi people or free the Middle East of Saddam Hussein.

Did Operation Iraqi Freedom accomplish these goals? Only time will tell. The final outcome of Operation Iraqi Freedom will not be known for many years. Months after the end of Hussein's rule, the country was still unstable. Those who remained loyal to Hussein continued to commit violent acts against coalition troops still in the country. It will take time to rebuild Iraq and help the people establish a new government there.

★ TIMELINE ★

1990—*July 21*: Satellite photos show Iraqi troops gathered near the border of Kuwait.

July 25: Ambassador April Glaspie meets with Saddam Hussein.

August 2: Iraqi troops invade Kuwait; United Nations Security Council passes Resolution 660, demanding withdrawal of Iraqi troops from Kuwait.

August 6: Schwarzkopf meets with Saudi Arabian King Fahd; Fahd asks for help from coalition to defend Saudi Arabia; United Nations Security Council passes Resolution 661, imposing economic sanctions against Iraq; Army 82nd Airborne is activated for Operation Desert Shield; United States ships *Independence* and *Eisenhower* ordered to Middle East.

August 7: U.S. ships *Saratoga* and *Wisconsin* leave United States for Persian Gulf.

August 8: F15 Eagle fighter jets and E-3 AWACS surveillance planes arrive in Saudi Arabia.

August 9: Army 82nd Airborne arrives in Saudi Arabia.

August 18: President Bush activates Civil Reserve Air Fleet to help transport men and equipment to Saudi Arabia.

August 24: Schwarzkopf moves his command headquarters to Saudi Arabia.

November 29: United Nations passes Resolution 678, authorizing the coalition to use "all means necessary" if Iraq is not out of Kuwait by January 15, 1991.

1991—*January 17*: Operation Desert Storm begins with bombing attack on Baghdad.

January 18: Iraq fires Scud missiles at Israel.

January 22: Iraqi troops begin attacks on Kuwaiti oil pumps and tankers, spilling millions of barrels of oil into Persian Gulf.

February 13: American fighter planes bomb Al-Firdos bunker in Baghdad, injuring hundreds of civilians.

February 16: Iraqi delegate to United Nations announces that his country will use weapons of mass destruction if the coalition continues to bomb Iraq.

February 22: Iraqi soldiers begin setting fire to Kuwaiti oil wells.

February 24: Coalition forces begin the ground war against Iraq.

February 25: Scud missile hits military barracks near Dhahran Airbase in Saudi Arabia, killing twenty-eight U.S. soldiers and wounding ninety-eight.

February 26: Coalition planes destroy hundreds of retreating Iraqi troops in vehicles along Highway 6, north of Basra; Reporters call Highway 6 the "Highway of Death"; In a speech on Iraqi radio, Saddam Hussein announces to the Iraqi people that Iraq has achieved victory over the coalition.

February 27: Joint Forces Command (JFC) made up of Saudi, Egyptian, and Syrian troops enters Kuwait to help residents celebrate their freedom from Iraqi occupation; On television in the United States, President George Bush announces that the coalition's war objectives have been achieved, and the fighting will end.

March 3: General Norman Schwarzkopf and coalition leaders meet with Iraqi generals to complete details of the cease-fire agreement.

March 5: Coalition prisoners of war released.

April: Iraqi troops attack Shiite Muslim towns and Kurdish villages in Iraq; Thousands of Kurds escape to Turkey; Coalition sends food and medical aid to Turkey to help Kurdish refugees.

June: Returning troops celebrate the coalition victory in Iraq in cities and towns across America.

2002—*November 25*: United Nations weapons inspectors arrive in Iraq to search for weapons of mass destruction.

2003—*March 19*: Operation Iraqi Freedom begins with bombing of specific targets in Baghdad (morning of March 20 in Iraq).

April 9: United States and allied leaders announce that the government of Saddam Hussein has fallen.

★ CHAPTER NOTES ★

Chapter 1. Baghdad Blasted

1. Hugh Grossman, e-mail to Debra McArthur, May 3, 2002.

2. Ibid.

3. Rick Atkinson, *Crusade: The Untold Story of the Persian Gulf War* (Boston: Houghton Mifflin Co., 1993), p. 15.

4. Ibid., p. 16.

5. Thomas B. Allen, F. Clifton Berry, and Norman Polmar. *War in the Gulf* (Atlanta, Ga.: Turner Publishing Inc., 1991), p. 126.

6. Grossman.

7. Anita Porter-Weldon, e-mail to Debra McArthur, April 3, 2002.

8. Michael R. Gordon and General Bernard E. Trainor, *The Generals' War: The Inside Story of the Conflict in the Gulf* (Boston: Little, Brown, and Co., 1994), pp. 209–210.

9. Ibid., pp. 215–216.

10. Richard Zoglin, "Live From the Middle East," *Time*, January 28, 1991, p. 70.

11. General H. Norman Schwarzkopf, *It Doesn't Take a Hero* (New York: Linda Grey Bantam Books, 1992), p. 415.

12. "How CNN Phoned Home," *Time*, January 28, 1991, p. 71.

13. Matthew Cooper, "The Very Nervy Win of CNN," *U.S. News and World Report*, January 28, 1991, p. 44.

14. Allen, et. al., p. 132.

15. Colonel Harvey D. Watson, e-mail to Debra McArthur, April 1, 2002.

16. Atkinson, p. 47.

17. Gordon and Trainor, p. 219.

Chapter 2. Rumors of War

1. Elaine Sciolino, *The Outlaw State: Saddam Hussein's Quest for Power and the Gulf Crisis* (New York: John Wiley and Sons, Inc., 1991), pp. 37–38.

2. Michael Palmer, *Guardians of the Gulf: A History of America's Expanding Role in the Persian Gulf, 1833–1992* (New York: Free Press, 1992), p. 13.

3. Sciolino, p. 39.

4. Ibid., p. 45.

5. Ibid.

6. Kenneth R. Timmerman, Death Lobby: How the West Armed Iraq (Boston: Houghton-Mifflin Co., 1991), pp. 16–18.

7. Ibid., p. 65.

8. Ibid., pp. 138–140.

9. Thomas B. Allen, F. Clifton Berry, and Norman Polmar, *War in the Gulf* (Atlanta: Turner Publishing Inc., 1991), p. 18.

10. Charles Lane, "Requiem for an Oil Kingdom," *Newsweek*, August 13, 1990, p. 24.

11. Allen, Berry, and Polmar, pp. 61–62.

12. Michael R. Gordon and General Bernard E. Trainor, *The Generals' War: The Inside Story of the Conflict in the Gulf* (Boston: Little, Brown, and Co., 1994), pp. 13–14, 19.

13. John R. MacArthur, *Second Front: Censorship and Propaganda in the Gulf War* (New York: Hill and Wang, 1992), p. 41.

14. Gordon and Trainor, p. 23.

15. General H. Norman Schwarzkopf, *It Doesn't Take a Hero* (New York: Linda Grey Bantam Books, 1992), pp. 293–294.

16. Brigadier General Robert H. Scales, *Certain Victory: The U. S. Army in the Gulf War* (Washington, D.C.: Brassey's, 1994), p. 45.

Chapter 3. Preparing for War

1. "The UN Acts," *UN Chronicle*, December 1990, p. 10.

2. Ibid.

3. Ibid., p. 9.

4. Ibid., p. 10.

5. Ibid., p. 11.

6. Lisa Beyer, "The World Closes In," *Time*, August 20, 1990, p. 26.

7. Jill Smolowe, "Me and My Brother Against My Cousin," *Time*, August 20, 1990, p. 33.

8. General H. Norman Schwarzkopf, *It Doesn't Take a Hero* (New York: Linda Grey Bantam Books, 1992), p. 305.

9. Brian Duffy, "The Guns of August," *U.S. News and World Report*, August 20, 1990, p. 20.

10. Thomas B. Allen, F. Clifton Berry, and Norman Polmar, *War in the Gulf* (Atlanta: Turner Publishing Inc., 1991), p. 97.

11. Brigadier General Robert H. Scales, *Certain Victory: The U.S. Army in the Gulf War* (Washington, D.C.: Brassey's, 1994), pp. 6–7.

12. Ibid., p. 7.

13. Ibid., p. 17.

14. Stephen Budiansky, "A Force Reborn," *U.S. News and World Report*, March 18, 1991, pp. 31–32.

15. Russell Watson and Gregg Easterbrook, "A New Kind of Warfare," *Newsweek*, January 28, 1991, p. 23.

16. William B. Scott, "Realistic Large-Force Training Prepares U.S. Army for Rigors of Desert Combat," *Aviation Week and Space Technology*, September 3, 1990, p. 171.

17. Schwarzkopf, p. 291.

18. Harvey Watson, e-mail to Debra McArthur, June 20, 2002.

19. Scales, p. 44.

20. Schwarzkopf, p. 305.

Chapter 4. Raising the Shield

1. Rhonda Cornum, *She Went to War* (Novato, Calif.: Presidio, 1992), p. 19.

2. Barbara Kantrowitz and Mike Mason, "The Soldier-Parent Dilemma," *Newsweek*, November 12, 1990, p. 84.

3. Cornum, p. 21.

4. General H. Norman Schwarzkopf, *It Doesn't Take a Hero* (New York: Linda Grey Bantam Books, 1992), p. 310.

5. Ibid., p. 341.

6. Brigadier General Robert H. Scales, *Certain Victory: The U.S. Army in the Gulf War* (Washington, D.C.: Brassey's, 1994), p. 49.

7. Colonel Harvey D. Watson, e-mail to Debra McArthur, June 20, 2002.

8. Schwarzkopf, p. 311.

9. James Ott, "Desert Shield Deployment Tests CRAF's Viability," *Aviation Week & Space Technology*, December 10, 1990, p. 32.

10. Scales, p. 42.

11. Ibid.

12. Ibid., p. 73.

13. Ibid.

14. Major Michael Donnelly, *Falcon's Cry: A Desert Storm Memoir* (Westport, Conn.: Praeger, 1998), p. 56.

15. Schwarzkopf, p. 324.

Chapter 5. Ready . . . Set . . . Wait

1. Rhonda Cornum, *She Went to War* (Novato, Calif.: Presidio, 1992), p. 24.

2. Hilary Mackenzie, "America Digs in for War," *Maclean's*, September 3, 1990, p. 25.

3. Brigadier General Robert H. Scales, *Certain Victory: The U.S. Army in the Gulf War* (Washington, D.C.: Brassey's, 1994), p. 80.

4. Jeff Moore, e-mail to Debra McArthur, April 15, 2002.

5. Hugh Grossman, e-mail to Debra McArthur, May 3, 2002.

6. Rick Atkinson, *Crusade: The Untold Story of the Persian Gulf War* (Boston: Houghton Mifflin, 1993), p. 74.

7. Stephen S. Arnon, et. al. "Botulinum Toxin as a Biological Weapon," *Journal of the American Medical*

Association, Vol 285, No. 8, February 28, 2001, p. 1059, <http://jama.ama-assn.org/cgi/content/full/286/8/1059?SEARCHID=1048099637881> (April 5, 2003).

8. Stanley W. Kandebo, "Western Manufacturers Say Powerplants Can Withstand Rigors of Mideast Climate," *Aviation Week and Space Technology*, August 20, 1990, pp. 25–26.

9. Jeff Moore, e-mail to Debra McArthur, April 15, 2002.

10. Ibid.

11. General H. Norman Schwarzkopf, *It Doesn't Take a Hero* (New York: Linda Grey Bantam Books, 1992), p. 423.

12. Ibid., p. 338.

13. *Conduct of the Persian Gulf Conflict: An Interim Report to Congress* (Washington, D.C.: U.S. Government Printing Office, 1991), pp. 10–11.

14. Anita Porter-Weldon, e-mail to Debra McArthur, April 3, 2002.

15. Michael Donnelly, *Falcon's Cry: A Desert Storm Memoir* (Westport, Conn.: Praeger, 1998), pp. 72–73.

16. Harvey Watson, e-mail to Debra McArthur, June 20, 2002.

17. Cornum, p. 35.

18. May Kay Cosmetics archives, e-mail to Debra McArthur, August 7, 2002.

19. Andrew Watson, e-mail to Debra McArthur, October 14, 2002.

20. Michael R. Gordon and General Bernard E. Trainor, *The Generals' War: The Inside Story of the Conflict in the Gulf* (Boston: Little, Brown, and Co., 1994), p. 182.

Chapter 6. War From the Air

1. Rick Atkinson, *Crusade: The Untold Story of the Persian Gulf War* (Boston: Houghton Mifflin Co., 1993), pp. 74–76.

2. *Conduct of the Persian Gulf Conflict: An Interim Report to Congress* (Washington, D.C.: U.S. Government Printing Office, 1991), pp. 25–31.

3. Thomas B. Allen, F. Clifton Berry, and Norman Polmar, *War in the Gulf* (Atlanta: Turner Publishing Inc., 1991), p. 132.

4. Kenneth R. Timmerman, *Death Lobby: How the West Armed Iraq* (Boston: Houghton-Mifflin Co., 1991), p. 149.

5. Ibid., pp. 287–288.

6. Atkinson, p. 145.

7. Ibid., p. 77.

8. Ibid., pp. 84–85.

9. Ibid., p. 91.

10. William L. Smallwood, *Strike Eagle: Flying the F-15E in the Gulf War* (Washington, D.C.: Brassey's, 1994), pp. 133–134.

11. *Conduct of the Persian Gulf Conflict*, pp. 13–21.

12. Sharon Begley, "Saddam's Ecoterror," *Newsweek*, February 4, 1991, p. 36.

13. Ibid., p. 38.

14. Ibid., p. 39.

15. Michael R. Gordon and General Bernard E. Trainor, *The Generals' War: The Inside Story of the Conflict in the Gulf* (Boston: Little, Brown, and Co., 1994), p. 326.

16. Atkinson, p. 159.

17. Lewis Lord, "The War's Other Front," *U.S. News and World Report*, February 4, 1991, p. 54.

18. Nancy Gibbs, "First Thick Shock of War," *Time*, January 28, 1991, p. 37.

19. *Conduct of the Persian Gulf Conflict*, pp. 19–21.

20. Allen, Berry, and Polmar, p. 155.

21. *Conduct of the Persian Gulf Conflict: An Interim Report to Congress* (Washington, D.C.: U.S. Government Printing Office, 1991), p. 19-1.

22. Harvey Watson, e-mail to Debra McArthur, October 14, 2002.

23. Gordon and Trainor, p. 230.

24. PBS Online and WGBH19, "Frontline: The Gulf War," *Weapons: Mim-104 Patriot*, <http://www.pbs.org/wgbh/pages/frontline/gulf/weapons/patriot.html> (April 20, 2003).

25. Atkinson, p. 79.

26. Ibid., pp. 181–182.

27. Gordon and Trainor, p. 322.

28. Jeff Moore, e-mail to Debra McArthur, April 15, 2002.

Chapter 7. One Hundred Hours to Victory

1. Rick Atkinson, *Crusade: The Untold Story of the Persian Gulf War* (Boston: Houghton Mifflin Co., 1993), p. 375.

2. Brigadier General Robert H. Scales, *Certain Victory: The U.S. Army in the Gulf War* (Washington, D.C.: Brassey's, 1994), p. 216.

3. Anita Porter-Weldon, e-mail to Debra McArthur, April 3, 2002.

4. Hugh Grossman, e-mail to Debra McArthur, May 16, 2002.

5. Scales, p. 219.

6. Ibid., p. 220.

7. Jeff Moore, e-mail to Debra McArthur, November 2, 2002.

8. Atkinson, p. 414.

9. Ibid., p. 416.

10. Ibid., pp. 418–420.

11. William L. Smallwood, *Strike Eagle: Flying the F-15E in the Gulf War* (Washington, D.C.: Brassey's, 1994), p. 189.

12. Jeff Moore.

13. Scales, p. 270.

14. Atkinson, pp. 466–468.

15. George Bush, "Cessation of Hostilities." Speech delivered to the American People February 27, 1991, *Vital Speeches of the Day*, March 15, 1991, p. 329.

16. General H. Norman Schwarzkopf, *It Doesn't Take a Hero* (New York: Linda Grey Bantam Books, 1992), p. 489.

17. Bush, p. 328.

18. Thomas B. Allen, F. Clifton Berry, and Norman Polmar, *War in the Gulf* (Atlanta: Turner Publishing Inc., 1991), p. 214.

19. General Michael Dugan, "First Lessons of Victory," *U.S. News and World Report*, March 18, 1991, pp. 32, 36.

Chapter 8. Incomplete Victory?

1. Saddam Hussein, "Iraq Withdrawal From Kuwait," A Speech Delivered on Baghdad Radio, February 26, 1991, *Vital Speeches of the Day*, March 15, 1991, p. 327.

2. Michael R. Gordon and General Bernard E. Trainor, *The Generals' War: The Inside Story of the Conflict in the Gulf* (Boston: Little, Brown, and Co., 1994), p. 459.

3. Rick Atkinson, *Crusade: The Untold Story of the Persian Gulf War* (Boston: Houghton Mifflin Co., 1993), p. 461.

4. Green Cross International, "An Environmental Assessment of Kuwait, Seven Years after the Gulf War," <http://www.cgi.ch/pdf/finalkuwait2.pdf>, pp. iii–iv (November 21, 2002).

5. Martin Yant, *Desert Mirage: The True Story of the Gulf War* (New York: Prometheus Books, 1991), p. 180.

6. Asaf Muhamad, letter to Debra McArthur, May 10, 2002.

7. Stephen Budiansky, "A Force Reborn," *U.S. News and World Report*, March 18, 1991, p. 30.

8. Ibid.

9. *Conduct of the Persian Gulf Conflict: An Interim Report to Congress* (Washington, D.C.: U.S. Government Printing Office, 1991), pp. 10–11.

10. James Walsh, "A Partnership to Remember" *Time*, March 11, 1991, p. 49.

11. John R. MacArthur, *Second Front: Censorship and Propaganda in the Gulf War* (New York: Hill and Wang, 1992), pp. 155–156.

12. PBS Online and WGBH19, "Frontline: The Gulf War," *Weapons: Mim-104 Patriot*, <http://www.pbs.org/wgbh/pages/frontline/gulf/weapons/patriot.html> (April 20, 2003).

13. Colonel David Hackworth, "Oops, More Unexpected Casualties," September 17, 2002, <http://www.gulfweb.org/doc_show.cfm?ID=762> (November 26, 2002).

14. William L. Smallwood, *Strike Eagle: Flying the F-15E in the Gulf War* (Washington, D.C.: Brassey's, 1994), p. 192.

15. Atkinson, p. 457.

16. Gordon and Trainor, p. 383.

17. Atkinson, p. 397.

18. Ibid., p. 88.

19. Ibid., p. 496.

20. Gordon and Trainor, p. 457.

21. "President Makes Appeal for Support," *Kansas City Star*, October 8, 2002, p. A1.

22. "Large Force Called for in Iraq Plan," *Kansas City Star*, November 1, 2002, p. A1.

23. "President Bush Addresses the Nation," Speech delivered March 19, 2003, <http://www.whitehouse.gov/news/release/2003/02/iraq/20030319-17.html> (April 23, 2003).

24. "Iraq Site Tests Positive for Toxic Nerve Agents," *Kansas City Star*, April 8, 2003, p. A1.

★ FURTHER READING ★

Books

Cornum, Rhonda. *She Went to War*. Novato, Calif.: Presidio, 1992.

Gay, Kathlyn and Martin K. Gay. *Persian Gulf War*. New York: Twenty-First Century Books, 1996.

Holden, Henry M. *The Persian Gulf War: A MyReportLinks.com Book*. Berkeley Heights, N.J.: Enslow Publishers, Inc., 2003.

Hossell, Karen Price. *The Persian Gulf War*. Chicago: Heinemann Library, 2003.

Kent, Zachary. *The Persian Gulf War: "The Mother of all Battles."* Hillside, N.J.: Enslow Publishers, Inc., 1994.

Speakman, Jay. *Weapons of War*. San Diego: Lucent Books, 2001.

Spencer, William. *Iraq: Old Land, New Nation in Conflict*. Brookfield, Conn.: Twenty-First Century Books, 2000.

Stein, Richard. *The Mideast After the Gulf War*. Brookfield, Conn.: Millbrook Press, 1992.

Video Recordings

BBC/WGBH Frontline. *The Gulf War*. Seattle, Wash.: PBS Video, 1996.

Lou Reda Productions, Inc. for the History Channel. *Desert Storm: The Ultimate War*. New York: A&E Television Networks, 1996.

★ INTERNET ADDRESSES ★

Desert Storm.com. n.d. <http://www.desertstorm.com>.

"The Gulf War Story." *GulfLINK*. n.d. <http://www.gulflink.osd.mil/story_gwi.html>.

PBS Online and WGBH. *Frontline: The Gulf War*. 1996, 2002. <http://www.pbs.org/wgbh/pages/frontline/gulf/>.

★ INDEX ★

A
Ahmed, Sultan Hashim, 94
al-Bakr, Ahmed Hassan, 23, 24
Al-Firdos bunker, 72–73
Al Khobar attack, 86–87, 89
amyotrophic lateral sclerosis (ALS), 103–104
anti-aircraft artillery (AAA), 12, 73
Apache helicopters, 11, 85, 91, 104
Arab League, 33–34
Arens, Moshe, 69
armored combat earth-movers (ACEs), 105

B
Baath party, 23
Baker, James A., III, 69
B-52 bombers, 17, 66
biological weapons, 9, 27, 56, 69, 105
British military, 15, 85, 90
Bush, George, 8, 30, 74, 80, 93–94, 98
Bush, George Walker, 106–108

C
Carter, Jimmy, 26, 37
Central Command (CENTCOM), 40, 45
chemical weapons, 9, 27, 56, 69, 105–106
Cheney, Dick, 34, 41, 93
Civilian Reserve Air Fleet (CRAF), 48, 49

coalition forces
aid to Shiites and Kurds, 98–99
in battle, 16, 66–68, 72–74, 80–86, 90–93
blockade by, 63
conduct, 104–105
cooperation, 15, 44, 59, 60–61, 79
formation, 34–35
in Operation Iraqi Freedom, 107
success, 94, 100–101
Cody, Dick, 11
Cornum, Rhonda, 43, 53, 61–62, 91

D
Defense Intelligence Agency (DIA), 30
Donnelly, Michael, 52, 61
Dugan, Michael, 94
Dwight D. Eisenhower, 47

E
EF-11A Ravens, 12
E-3 Airborne Warning and Control System (AWACS), 10–11, 47

F
Fahd Bin Abdul Aziz Al-Saud, King 34–35, 41, 44
Faisal I, King, 19, 21
Federal Express (FedEx), 48
F-15E, 47, 78, 89
F-111F, 78
F-117A Stealth fighter-bombers, 12, 16

Forward-Looking Infrared Radar System (FLIRS), 11, 78, 90
Forward Operating Base (FOB), 81, 85
Franks, Tommy, 107
French military, 15, 24, 85

G
Glaspie, April, 30
Green Cross International (GCI), 97–98
Grossman, Hugh, 7, 9, 54–55, 84
Gulf War Syndrome, 102–104

H
"Highway of Death," 88–89, 93, 104
Highway 8, 85–88
Highway 6. *See* Highway of Death.
Hitler, Adolf, 22
Horner, Charles, 16, 41
hostages, 42, 64–65
Hussein, Saddam, 23–24, 28, 34, 52, 67–70, 96, 98–99 106, 108

I
Identification Friend or Foe (IFF), 15
Independence, 47
Instant Thunder, 10–16, 65, 66
Internal Look, 40, 43
Iran, 18, 24, 26–28, 36
Iraq
    occupation of Kuwait, 28–33, 60, 61, 63, 96
    war with Iran, 26–28

Israel, 22, 29, 68–70, 77, 101, 102
Italian military, 15, 61

J
Joint Forces Command (JFC), 81, 83, 91, 101
Joint Surveillance Target Attack Radar System (JSTARS), 88
Jones, Dave, 11

K
Khomeini, Ayatollah Ruhallah, 26
Kuwait, 7, 15, 17, 28, 30–31, 42, 45
Kuwaiti Theatre of Operations (KTO), 81, 83, 86

M
Meals, Ready to Eat (MREs), 51, 61
Military Airlift Command (MAC), 52
Mirage F1, 24
M-1A1, 90, 91
Moore, Jeff, 55, 57, 78–79, 85, 89
Muhamad, Asaf, 98–99
Muslims
    Kurds, 21, 22, 28, 98–99
    Shiites, 19, 21, 22, 26, 98
    Sunni, 19, 21, 22

N
National Training Center (NTC), 39
nuclear weapons, 29, 64–65, 69, 105–106

O

oil, 70–72, 75, 83
Operation Dear Abby, 63
Operation Iraqi Freedom,
 107–108

P

Pagonis, William, 44
Party of Arab Resistance. *See*
 Baathist Party.
Patriot missile, 38, 68,
 76–78, 87, 102
Paul F. Foster, 8
Persia. *See* Iran.
Porter, Anita, 9–10, 60, 84
Powell, Colin, 31, 93
prisoners of war (POWs),
 73–74, 84, 94, 95
Psychological Operations
 (PSYOPS), 83–84

R

Reagan, Ronald, 26, 37
REFORGER, 44
Republican Guard, 27, 30,
 31, 81, 85, 86, 90, 91
Resolution 678, 64
Resolution 660, 32
Resolution 661, 33

S

Saddam Hussein. *See*
 Hussein, Saddam.
Saratoga, 47
Saudi Arabian military, 15,
 44–45
Schwarzkopf, H. Norman,
 13–14, 16, 31, 34, 43,
 52, 66, 93–94, 100

Scuds, 67–68, 70, 76–78,
 86–87
"smart" bomb, 38
Speicher, Scott, 16
Strategic Air Campaign
 (SAC), 66–67
surface-to-air-missiles
 (SAMs), 73
Sykes-Picot Agreement,
 19, 20

T

tank plinking, 78, 80
Tomahawk Land Attack
 Missiles (TLAMs), 7–8,
 13, 14, 66
T-72 tanks, 86, 90, 91, 103

U

United Arab Emirates
 (UAE), 29
United Nations (UN), 32–33,
 34, 42, 64, 106
United Parcel Service
 (UPS), 48
U.S.S. Mississippi, 63–64
U.S.S. Wisconsin, 8, 47

V

Vietnam War, 35–36,
 100–102

W

Watson, Andrew, 63–64, 76
Watson, Harvey D., 16, 41,
 47–48, 61
weapons inspections, 106
Whitley, Al, 16–17

Y

Yeosock, John, 45, 46